The ICSA
Director's Guide

2ND EDITION

Martha Bruce

Published by ICSA Publishing Ltd
16 Park Crescent
London
WIB IAH

© ICSA Publishing Ltd 2004
    Reprinted 2006

Typeset in Sabon & ITC Franklin Gothic by
Paul Barrett Book Production, Cambridge

Printed and bound in Great Britain by
Marston Book Services Limited, Oxford

British Library Cataloguing in Publication Data

A catalogue record for this book is available from the British Library.

ISBN 1-86072-247-4

Contents

Introduction

Whilst there are a number of books to help directors understand the consequences of their appointment, I was delighted when I was asked to write this book for ICSA. I have felt for a long time that it would be very useful for directors to have a pocket-sized publication to carry with them and use as a quick reference. To achieve this I have written this guide in a concise and easy to read manner so directors and those who advise them can easily find the information they need about their duties, responsibilities and what is required of them.

As well as explaining the facts about the appointment of directors, their powers and how they are exercised in managing the company, the guide also covers directors' core duties and responsibilities in terms of administration, disclosure requirements, restricted transactions, financial accounts and shareholders. It also addresses increasingly important responsibilities for directors in the wider context towards employees, customers, creditors and the environment, commonly referred to as 'corporate social responsibility', which has received much press coverage and government attention in recent years.

Whilst it is not possible to cover all these areas in detail within this book, my aim has been to provide directors with essential information enabling them to refer elsewhere for more detail as required.

Given the extent of their duties, directors face a difficult task of making sure they stay up-to-date with changes in legislation and commercial practice. Not least amongst these are the changes that are expected to arise from the Company Law Review, which will be included in future editions as they take effect, and from implementing corporate governance recommendations described in the Combined Code 2003 and associated reports, evaluation of the board's performance, money laundering requirements, directors' remuneration report regulations and provisions of the Enterprise Act 2002 explained in this edition.

Writing such a concise guide for directors has proved challenging and I hope the reader finds it a useful addition to his or her briefcase.

While every effort has been made to ensure the accuracy of this work, neither the author nor the publisher can accept responsibility for any loss arising to anyone relying on the information contained therein.

MARTHA BRUCE FCIS
PARTNER, DAVID VENUS & COMPANY

Abbreviations

AIM	The Alternative Investment Market of the Stock Exchange
CA 1985	Companies Act 1985 (as amended)
CA 1989	Companies Act 1989
CDDA 1986	Company Directors Disqualification Act 1986
CJA 1993	Criminal Justice Act 1993
COMAH	Control of Major Accidents Hazards Regulations 1999 (SI 1999/743)
COSHH 1999	Control of Substances Hazardous to Health Regulations 1999
CPA 1987	Consumer Protection Act 1987
DDA 1995	Disability Discrimination Act 1995
DPA 1998	Data Protection Act 1998
EA 1995	Environment Act 1995
ELCIA 1969	Employers Liability (Compulsory Insurance) Act 1969
ENA 2002	Enterprise Act 2002
EPA 1990	Environmental Protection Act 1990
ERA 1996	Employment Rights Act 1996
ERDRA 1998	Employment Rights (Dispute Resolution) Act 1998
FRC	Financial Reporting Council
FSMA 2000	Financial Services and Markets Act 2000
FTA 1973	Fair Trading Act 1973
HSE	Health and Safety Executive
HSWA 1974	Health and Safety at Work, etc Act 1974
IA 1986	Insolvency Act 1986
IA 2000	Insolvency Act 2000
EO	Enforcement Order
ICAEW	Institute of Chartered Accountants in England & Wales
ICSA	Institute of Chartered Secretaries and Administrators
NAPF	National Association of Pension Funds
OPRA	Occupational Pensions Regulatory Authority
OFR	Operating and Financial Review
OFT	Office of Fair Trading
PIRC	Pensions Investment Research Consultants Ltd
POCA 2002	Proceeds of Crime Act 2002
POS	Public Offers of Securities Regulations 1995 SI 1995/19237
Registrar	Registrar of Companies (unless context implies otherwise)
SAS 600	Statement of Auditing Standards 600, Auditors' reports on financial statements
Schedule	Schedule to the Companies Acts
SDA 1975	Sex Discrimination Act 1975
Stock Exchange	The London Stock Exchange
TDA 1968	Trades Descriptions Act 1968

Glossary

The following explanations are not intended to be strict legal definitions.

Administrator A person appointed by the court to manage a company in financial difficulties in order to protect creditors and, if possible, avoid liquidation. The administrator has the power to remove and appoint directors.

Agent Someone who is authorised to carry out business transactions on behalf of another (the principal) who is thereby bound by such actions.

Annual general meeting (AGM) A general meeting of the company's members which must be held in each calendar year within 15 months of the previous AGM. See also *General meeting. Extraordinary general meeting.*

Articles Articles of Association, a constitutional document setting out the internal regulations of the company. Unless modified or excluded, the specimen articles in Table A have effect. See also *Table A.*

Board (of directors) See *Director.*

Case law The principles and rules of law established by judicial decisions. Under this system the decision reached in a particular case creates a precedent: that is, it is regarded as exemplifying rules of broader application which must be followed except by higher courts. See also *Common law.*

Class rights The rights attached to different classes of shares.

Combined Code 2003 The Combined Code issued by the Financial Reporting Council and applying to reporting years beginning on or after 1 November 2003.

Common law A body of law based on custom and usage and decisions reached in previous cases. The principles and rules of common law derive from judgments and judicial opinions delivered in response to specific circumstances, not from written legislation. See also *Case law, Statute law.*

Company secretary An officer of the company with a number of statutory duties, such as to sign the annual return and accompanying documents, and usually charged with a range of duties relating to the company's statutory books and records, filing requirements, etc. Every company must have a secretary who, in the case of a public company, must meet the qualification requirements laid down in the Companies Act.

Connected person Includes the spouse, child or stepchild of a director or any business partner or company associated with the director in which he or she has 20% of the equity share capital (CA 1985, s346).

Department of Trade and Industry The government department responsible for the administration of company law. The Companies Act confers certain powers on the Secretary of State for Trade and Industry.

Director An officer of the company responsible for determining policy, supervising the management of the company's business and exercising the powers of the company. Directors must generally carry out these functions collectively as a board.

Dividends The distribution of a portion of the company's profits to members according to the class and amount of their shareholdings.

Elective resolution A resolution, of which 21 days' notice has been given, approved unanimously by the members of the company entitled to vote.

Extraordinary general meeting (EGM) Any general meeting of the company's members that is not an annual general meeting. See also *Annual general meeting, General meeting.*

Extraordinary resolution A resolution approved by 75% of votes cast in general meeting.

General meeting A meeting of the company which all members (subject to restrictions in the Memorandum and Articles) are entitled to attend. See also *Annual general meeting, Extraordinary general meeting.*

Insider dealing Buying or selling shares on the basis of an unfair advantage derived from access to price-sensitive information not generally available.

Liquidation The process under which a company ceases to trade and realises its assets for distribution to creditors and then shareholders. The term 'winding up' is synonymous.

Listed company A company whose shares are dealt on the Official List of the London Stock Exchange.

Listing Rules Published by the UK Listing Authority, these detail the requirements that must be met by companies before their shares can be dealt with on the Official List of the Stock Exchange. For the full requirements, readers should refer to and rely only on the latest edition, available from the UK Listing Authority.

Material interest Any interest other than one where a person is managing investments for another or is operating an authorised unit trust, recognised trust or collective investment scheme; belongs to an open-ended investment company; or where the person is trustee or nominee for another (see CA 1985, s199(2A) for the full definition).

Memorandum Memorandum of Association, a constitutional document governing the company's relationship with the world at large, stating its name, domicile, objects, limitations of liability (if applicable) and authorised share capital.

Misfeasance Improper performance of a lawful action.

Non-cash asset Any property or interest in property other than cash and includes discharge of a person's liability and creation of an interest in property such as a lease (CA 1985, s739).

Officer Includes a director, manager or secretary of a company. An officer must have a level of supervisory control that reflects the general policy of the company, so not everyone with the title of manager is sufficiently senior to be regarded as an officer.

Ordinary resolution A resolution approved by a simple majority of votes cast in general meeting.

Ordinary shares The most common form of share in a company, giving holders the right to share in the company's profits in proportion to their holdings and the right to vote at general meetings (although non-voting ordinary shares are occasionally encountered).

Preference shares Shares carrying the right to payment of a fixed dividend out of profits before the payment of an ordinary dividend or the preferential return of capital or both.

Prohibited name In relation to appointment of a director, this means a name for a company which is the same as or similar to the name of a company that went into insolvent liquidation at any time within 12 months of the person being a director (refer to IA 1986, s216 (1) and (2) for the full definition).

Prospectus Any prospectus, notice, circular, advertisement or other invitation to the public to subscribe for or purchase a company's shares or debentures.

Proxy A person authorised by a member to vote on his or her behalf at a general meeting.

Quasi-loan Where one party makes payment to another or incurs expenditure on their behalf without an agreement but on the understanding that the money will be repaid (see CA 1985, s33 1(3) for the full definition).

Registered office The address at which legal documents may be served on the company and where the statutory books are normally kept. The registered office need not be the company's place of business and may be changed freely so long as it remains in the country of origin.

Registrar of companies The official responsible for maintaining the company records filed under the requirements of the Companies Act.

Relevant company A public or a private company in a group structure in which another company is a public company (CA 1985, s 331(6)).

Return date Either the anniversary of incorporation or the anniversary of the date shown on the previous year's annual return.

Secretary of State Within this book, refers to the Secretary of State for Trade and Industry.

Special resolution A resolution, of which 21 days' notice has been given, approved by 75% of votes cast in general meeting.

Statute law The body of law represented by legislation, and thus occurring in authoritative written form. Statute law contrasts with common law, over which it takes precedence.

Statutory books The general term applied to the registers and minute books that the Companies Act requires a company to maintain.

Subscriber A person who subscribes to the Memorandum and agrees to take up shares in the company on incorporation.

Table A The specimen articles of association for a company limited by shares set out in the Companies (Tables A to F) Regulations 1985. Unless specifically modified or excluded, the version of Table A in force at the time of a company's incorporation automatically applies to the company. A significantly revised version of Table A was intro-duced on 1 July 1985, but companies incorporated earlier are not affected unless they specifically adopt its provisions.

Turnbull Report The report *Internal Control: Guidance for Directors on the Combined Code* issued in September 1999 by the Turnbull Working Party.

Tyson Report The Tyson Report on the Recruitment and Development of Non-Executive Directors (June 2003) commissioned by the Department of Trade and Industry.

Written resolution Allows private companies to move any resolution without holding a general meeting. The written resolution must be signed by all members entitled to vote.

1   Fundamentals about directors

Most of this book is devoted to making sure directors are fully aware of their obligations. However, before considering these responsibilities directors need to understand a number of fundamental facts, covered in this chapter, which include:

- What they are
- Why they are needed
- How they are appointed
- Who can be appointed
- Types of director
- What happens if a director has not been formally appointed.

What is a director?

The only guidance given in the CA 1985 is that a director is 'any person occupying the position of director by whatever name called' (s741(1)). Consequently a director is not recognised by title, which may be governor, trustee, councillor, etc. but by the functions carried out.

Why does a company need directors?

Because a company is a separate legal entity, it can only operate through its directors and officers; it cannot act on its own. Therefore a private company cannot be incorporated unless it has at least one director, appointed in the first instance by the subscribers to the Memorandum, whilst a public company must have at least two (CA 1985, s282).

How are directors appointed?

As mentioned above, the first directors are appointed by the subscribers to the Memorandum when the company is incorporated (CA 1985, s10). The manner in which subsequent appointments are made is usually determined by provisions in the company's Articles, which may permit:

- the directors to appoint additional directors or to fill casual vacancies (Table A, Reg 79);
- the members to appoint directors by ordinary resolution (Table A, Reg 78);
- appointment by notice from the holding company where the company is a wholly-owned subsidiary;
- appointment by a holder of a particular class of share where, for example, the company is a joint venture and each party holds a different class of shares and has the right to appoint one director.

In each case the actual process will also be specified in the Articles and, where there is no mention of subsequent appointments in the Articles, the authority will be inferred on the members.

When a director is appointed, an entry needs to be made in the register of directors (see Chapter 6) and notification, including the director's consent, must be sent to Companies House within 14 days, using prescribed Form 288a. Where a director is at serious risk of violence or intimidation and this risk is demonstrable, it is permissible for the notification to Companies House to contain only a 'service' address whilst details of the director's home address are kept on a secure register (The Companies (Particulars of Usual Residential Address) (Confidentiality Orders) Regulations 2002).

The appointment will also give rise to various administrative matters, including notifying the company's bankers, amending the bank mandate instructions and informing the company's insurers.

Any change in a director's details, for example a change of address or a change of name through marriage, need to be noted in the company's register of directors and sent to Companies House using the prescribed Form 288c.

Who can be appointed a director?

The CA 1985 does not specify any qualifications for directors and most persons and legal entities can hold the position. Exceptions are someone who is:

- an undischarged bankrupt without leave of the court to act;
- subject to a disqualification order or has given a voluntary disqualification undertaking;

- prohibited for failing to pay amounts owing under a county court administration order;
- a director of an insolvent company and the proposed appointment is to a company with a 'prohibited name';
- secretary of the company and the appointment is as sole director;
- the auditor of the company;
- over 70 years of age and the appointment is as director of a public company and neither the company's Articles nor the members by ordinary resolution have excluded this provision.

Furthermore, a person may be prohibited from appointment by provisions specified in the company's Articles, such as not having the requisite shareholding qualification, being a minor, suffering from mental disorder, or having entered into an arrangement with creditors.

What types of director are there?

Once someone has been formally appointed a director, the CA 1985 makes no distinction between them according to their role or title. Consequently all directors have the same statutory duties and obligations and have responsibility for participating in the joint deliberations of the board.

However, in accordance with principles of good corporate governance, companies often make a distinction between directors who have 'executive' status and those who act as 'non-executive' directors. Also, the directors are often permitted by the Articles to appoint an 'alternate director'. Whilst it makes no difference in terms of the CA 1985, the distinctions for the company and the directors are as follows.

i Executive directors

Full-time working directors are often described as 'executive directors'. In most instances they have service contracts with the company which, as well as their employment details, will set out their executive and management functions such as responsibility for production, finance, marketing, human resources and health and safety, and will often be given titles such as 'finance director', 'marketing director' and so forth. They will typically possess qualifications and experience relevant to their specialist function.

ii Non-executive directors

Directors who are not employees of the company and who only have to devote part of their time to its affairs as independent advisors or supervisors are often referred to as 'non-executive directors'. A non-executive director will not have an executive function nor be involved in the company's day-to-day management.

Whilst a non-executive director has the same statutory duties and obligations as any other director, past cases of disqualification have shown that in some instances the court expects a different and often lower standard of skill and care from non-executive directors. For example, in *Re Stephenson Cobbold Ltd [2001] BCC 38* the court refused to disqualify a non-executive director who, whilst he was a cheque signatory, was not involved in deciding who should be paid where preferential treatment of creditors had occurred.

Non-executive directors are considered necessary to:

- balance the interests of shareholders with those of management;
- bring independent judgement to decisions on strategy, performance, use of resources and appointments, etc.;
- mediate over issues in which executive directors may have a personal interest such as directors' remuneration, succession and takeovers, etc.;
- monitor performance and ensure sufficient safeguards and controls are in place to protect the interests of the company.

However, the effectiveness and need for non-executive directors has come under a great deal of scrutiny in the wake of large-scale corporate collapses including Enron, Marconi, Worldcom, Railtrack, Equitable Life and Independent Insurance. In response to this concern, the Secretary of State for Trade and Industry set up an independent review of the role and effectiveness of non-executive directors. Key recommendations to improve effectiveness made by Derek Higgs in the resulting report entitled *Review of the Role And Effectiveness of Non-Executive Directors* ('Higgs Review') are summarised in the table on page 14.

Many of the recommendations in the Higgs Review have been incorporated in the Combined Code 2003, set out in Appendix I. By implementing these recommendations it is intended that non-executive directors will be more effective and make a greater contribution, thereby improving the overall performance of the board.

Following publication of the Higgs Review, the Tyson Report into the recruitment and development of non-executive directors concluded that UK companies would benefit from greater diversity amongst non-executive directors and by adopting more rigorous and transparent recruiting procedures for them.

iii Alternate directors

Whilst there is no provision in the CA 1985, it is common practice for a company's Articles to allow executive or non-executive directors to appoint an 'alternate director' to attend and vote at meetings of the directors on their behalf (Table A, Reg 65). Provisions in the Articles will need to be carefully checked as the manner and procedure for appointment of an alternate director can vary considerably.

Alternate directors are subject to all statutory obligations and responsibilities of other directors. They must therefore have their details recorded in the register of directors and at Companies House and make disclosures to the company in terms of interests in shares and contracts, etc.

What if a director has not been formally appointed?

There are a number of instances where this may happen, whether by intention or by error. These include circumstances where the director would be referred to as the following.

i De facto director

This describes a person who assumes to act as a director, is held out by the company as a director and who claims to be a director without having been formally appointed to the board or whose appointment is later found to be improper *(Re Hydrodam (Corby) Ltd [1994] 2 BCLC 180, [1994] BCC 161)*.

Such a person is considered to have been a director, if not in name then in fact, and consequently is subject to the same responsibilities that apply to properly appointed directors. Furthermore, a de facto director whose conduct is considered 'unfit' under CDDA 1986, s6 *(Re Sykes (Butchers) Ltd (in liquidation), Secretary of State for Trade and Industry v Richardson [1998] 1 BCLC 110)* may be disqualified as a director.

Particular care should be taken when bestowing a courtesy title such as 'divisional' or 'regional' director on a senior executive. Such practice is not recommended as it causes confusion, often to the detriment of the company, and the person may be considered a de facto director. For example, in *SMC Electronics Limited v Akhter Computers Ltd [2001] 1 BCLC 433* an employee who was not a director but had the title 'Director of Power Supply Unit Sales' bound the company to a contract that could not be repudiated as the third party had reasonably assumed the employee had authority to enter into it.

ii Shadow director

CA 1985, s741 (2) defines a 'shadow director' as 'a person in accordance with whose instructions or directions the directors are accustomed to act'. This may, for example, include a majority shareholder, secured creditor or banker who, whilst not actually appointed a director, exercises influence over the affairs of the company and decisions made by the board *(Secretary of State for Trade and Industry v Deverell [2000] 2 All ER 365)*.

There are instances where, for example, a class of shareholders may have authority either expressed in the company's Articles or in a shareholders' agreement to appoint and remove a 'nominee' director. Whilst in principle there is nothing wrong with appointing someone as director in this way, that person must be left to exercise his or her own judgement in the best interests of the company without any direction or instruction on how to vote by the appointor *(Boulting v ACTT [1963] 2 QB 606, 626, CA)*. Where this is not the case, the appointor will be considered a shadow director.

To ensure that people who control companies but avoid appointment as directors do not evade their legal duties and responsibilities, shadow directors are subject to the same rules as properly appointed directors. Where their conduct falls below that reasonably expected of a director, shadow directors may be the subject of disqualification or be caught by wrongful trading provisions. They can also be liable for a breach of their fiduciary duties to the company *(Yukong Line Ltd of Korea v Rendsburg Investment Corp of Liberia and Others [1998] 2 BCLC 485)*.

Where it is apparent that a company has a shadow director, the situation should be regularised by formally appointing that person as a director.

2   Directors' powers and company management

As explained in Chapter 1, the authority by which directors act on behalf of companies is conferred on them collectively, therefore they must meet to discuss matters and make decisions. Where it is not possible for the directors to attend to all matters personally, they will need to delegate responsibility for particular tasks.

This chapter addresses how directors exercise their powers and 'manage' the affairs of the company efficiently and effectively, by covering:

- Directors' powers
- Board meetings
- Delegation of authority
- Corporate governance recommendations
- Evaluation of performance.

Corporate governance recommendations are addressed here as they are largely concerned with improving the way directors manage companies at the same time as increasing accountability for decisions made.

Directors' powers

A company's Articles will usually entrust the directors to manage the company and its business. For example, Table A, Reg 70 provides that 'the business of the company shall be managed by the directors who may exercise all the powers of the company'.

However, many companies' Articles, and indeed those in Table A, often restrict the extent of this authority by requiring that any limitations specified in the Companies Acts, Memorandum and Articles or special resolutions approved by the members are also observed. For example, whilst the directors usually have authority to enter into contracts on behalf of the company, the Articles may specify an upper limit to the value of such contracts and require that members' approval be sought where a contract exceeds this value.

Whilst a company's Articles generally authorise the directors to manage its business as described above, it is important to note that the directors do not have the power to act individually unless powers and responsibilities have been specifically delegated to them by the board. Consequently, directors must make decisions collectively as a board and act in accordance with the decisions made *(Re Haycraft Gold Reduction and Mining Co [1900] 2 Ch 230).*

Where the CA 1985 and other statutes state that the 'directors' have authority or are required to do something, in most instances this refers to all the directors acting together, not to individual directors. So, for example, where the directors have authority under CA 1985, s80 to allot shares, an allotment can only take place when decided by the board and not on the instruction of an individual director.

Board meetings

Apart from requiring minutes of all meetings of the board to be kept (CA 1985, s382), statutory provisions are silent about how board meetings are convened and carried out.

Similarly, although a company's Articles often contain some provisions governing board meetings, it is not uncommon for them to give the directors a large degree of freedom to call and conduct board meetings as they consider appropriate. For example, Table A, Reg 88 provides that the directors 'may regulate their meetings as they see fit'.

ICSA's best practice guide *Good Boardroom Practice* offers further guidance in this area.

In practice, private and public companies with larger boards tend to hold regular, scheduled and formal board meetings, as they are necessary to address the many facets of their operations and ensure the directors have the necessary information on which to base decisions. In contrast, directors of smaller companies tend to be more closely involved with day-to-day operations and less frequent and informal board meetings often suffice. Furthermore, smaller companies with, say, only two or three directors, generally find it easier to call impromptu board meetings to consider matters as they arise or to arrange for matters to be approved by resolution in writing.

A director has a general duty to attend board meetings when possible, but this does not mean every meeting *(Re City Equitable Fire Insurance Co Ltd [1925] Ch 407, CA).* However, someone who accepts appointment as a director must be willing and prepared to attend most, if not all, board meetings. The Articles will frequently provide that a director who fails to attend board meetings for a number of consecutive months, without permission from the board for the absence, shall be removed (Table A, Reg 81). The reasoning behind such provision is quite clear: a person who is never present at board meetings cannot be involved in and contribute to discharging the directors' responsibility to manage the company. Indeed, principle A.6 of the Combined Code 2003 (see Appendix 1) recommends that evaluation of the board's performance takes account of the commitment of time to board and committee meetings and other duties of the director.

It is always necessary to consult and observe provisions in the Articles concerning the conduct of board meetings when calling and holding a meeting. The following general principles may provide additional guidance, especially where the Articles are silent on any particular matter:

Notice	• All directors must be given notice of a board meeting unless excluded by the Articles, for example when absent from the UK (Table A, Reg 88).
	• Where board meetings are held at a fixed venue at regular pre-determined intervals, it may not be necessary to give notice of each meeting.
	• Where the Articles do not specify the length of notice required then 'reasonable' notice must be given, based largely on what is normal practice for the company.
	• Unless required by the Articles, notice does not need to set out details of the business to be considered but, from a practical point, the benefits of including this information are clear.
Attendance	• No director can be lawfully excluded from a board meeting (*Pulbrook v Richmond Consolidated Mining Co (1878) 9 Ch D 610*).
Quorum	• Where the required quorum is not present, the board meeting cannot proceed.
	• Where the articles do not specify what constitutes a quorum it will be a majority, unless the board's usual practice is a different number (*York Tramways Co v Willows (1882) 8 QBD 685, CA*).
	• The articles may allow the board to determine the quorum (Table A, Reg 89).

- Where a private company has only one director, then the sole director can constitute a quorum.
- The Articles may state that a director may be excluded from being counted in the quorum at a particular point in a meeting, for example where a director has an interest in a contract under discussion (Table A, Regs 94 and 95), and a check must be made that the meeting is remains quorate.

Conduct and voting
- The chair (appointed in accordance with provisions in the Articles) has responsibility to ensure the board meeting is conducted properly, preserve order and guide the directors through the business of the meeting, making sure that all matters are adequately discussed and decisions reached.
- Decisions of the board are usually decided by simple majority, and each director is entitled to one vote, unless the Articles specify something different.
- The chair only has a casting vote where provided by the Articles.

Minutes
- Minutes must be kept of all board meetings (CA 1985, s382).
- All decisions taken at the meeting must be recorded in the minutes, with a short explanatory narrative where necessary.

On some occasions it may not be possible to arrange for all directors to be present at one location to hold a board meeting, due to constraints of time or availability. Whilst there is no specific statutory provision, many companies have amended their Articles to allow:
- directors to hold meetings by telephone or similar electronic media, such as video conferencing;
- decisions of the board to be recorded by resolutions in writing signed by all directors (Table A, Reg 93).

Where directors' meetings are held by telephone, unless the Articles specifically provide for it, a series of telephone calls on a one-to-one basis stretches the common law meeting too far and is unlikely to be permitted. Consequently, it must be possible for directors to speak and be heard by the other directors at the 'meeting'.

Board meetings provide the ideal opportunity for directors to discuss the company's strategy and direction away from the day-to-day distractions of running the company. In most instances an agenda setting out the matters to be discussed will be prepared and circulated to the directors, accompanied by necessary supporting documents and papers such as monthly management accounts, sales figures, budget reports, draft agreements for consideration, etc. This formal approach enables the directors to come to the meeting prepared and in full knowledge of the facts necessary to reach decisions. In most instances this can improve the effectiveness and efficiency of board meetings. The alternative is to use the meeting as an opportunity to bring the directors up to speed with developments and then to expect them to make decisions at the end of the meeting, which may not allow adequate time for consideration. Many boards are moving away from this approach as it is not a very efficient use of their limited meeting time.

Delegation of authority

Except where the company is very small and the directors are effectively the operational managers of the business, it is unlikely they would be able to attend personally to all matters that concern the board. Where this is the case the directors can delegate responsibility for carrying out certain tasks. However, they must ensure that such persons have the necessary knowledge, experience, skills and understanding to carry out the tasks properly as the board will remain ultimately responsible for their actions. ICSA has published the guidance notes *Matters Reserved for the Board* to assist directors in determining what can be delegated.

In practice, the board will often delegate authority to the following.

i Committees

The company's Articles usually empower the directors to delegate their powers to committees consisting of one or more directors and to impose regulations by which such committees operate (Table A, Reg 72). However, where the Articles are silent on this matter, the directors have no such power of delegation.

The board resolution establishing a committee must be carefully drafted to ensure the committee's status and functions are clearly defined. For example, it must be clear whether the committee has been authorised to reach decisions and put them into effect itself or merely to consider a range of options and make recommendations to the board. To achieve this, 'terms of reference' setting out the committee's structure, membership, constitution, role and requirements for meetings and other matters would usually be determined and approved by the board. Terms of reference would typically include:

- details of and requirements for membership;
- details of how meetings are to be conducted in relation to the quorum, frequency, notice required and recording of minutes;
- duties of the committee;
- the authority of the committee and details of any limitations on the powers delegated by the board.

Committees frequently found in companies' management structures include audit, remuneration and nomination as well as share allotment and standing committees and those set up on an ad hoc basis to consider specific issues such as risk management, health and safety, environmental issues, acquisitions or disposals, etc.

ICSA has issued guidance notes containing model terms of reference for audit, remuneration and nomination committees, copies of which are available at *www.icsa.org.uk* and directors of listed companies should also refer to recommendations set out in the Combined Code 2003 (see Appendix 1).

The board can revoke any delegation of powers at any time by recording the decision in the board meeting minutes.

ii Managing or other director

It is usual for provisions in a company's Articles to permit the board to appoint a 'managing director' and for the board to confer any or all of its powers of management to the appointee (Table A, Regs 84 and 72) by simple resolution. This is often necessary for practical reasons where the board meets formally only, say, once or twice a month and day-to-day matters need to be approved in the meantime. Where this is an issue, the board may delegate authority to the managing director, for example to enter into contracts or agreements on behalf of the company, either generally or limited to certain transactions.

A company's Articles may also allow the directors to delegate such of their powers as they consider fit and desirable to any director holding another executive office (Table A, Reg 72). For example, the operations directors may be delegated authority for signing commercial contracts on behalf of the company up to a specified monetary limit without need for formal board approval each time.

iii Agents

Table A, Reg 71 permits the directors to appoint any person, by power of attorney or otherwise, to be the agent of the company for such purposes and on such conditions as they determine. For example where presence in person is required overseas, delegation of power to an agent may be used, with the solicitor or attorney who represents the company acting as appointed agent.

iv Company secretary

At present all companies are required to appoint a company secretary. In practice, the directors delegate many tasks of a legal and compliance nature as well as relying on the secretary for technical, legal, compliance, management or administrative advice.

Whilst company secretaries' roles vary tremendously, in many cases they assist the directors by:

- advising them of the requirement to act in the best interests of the company and to be able to demonstrate that they have done so;
- keeping them aware of their responsibilities towards shareholders, employees, creditors and other stakeholders and the implications of decisions on these other parties;
- ensuring compliance with legal, Stock Exchange or contractual requirements;
- properly recording decisions of the board;
- informing directors of their obligations and assisting with information disclosed.

However, whilst responsibilities may be delegated to the company secretary to the extent indicated above, the directors remain ultimately responsible for ensuring that all legal requirements are being met. It is therefore important that directors periodically check the company secretary is carrying out delegated tasks satisfactorily.

The importance of the company secretary in a company's management was endorsed by inclusion in the Combined Code 2003 (see Appendix 1, A.5.3) of the requirement that 'all directors should have access to the advice and services of the company secretary who is responsible to the board for ensuring that board procedures are complied with'.

Corporate governance recommendations

REPORT	KEY RECOMMENDATIONS
Cadbury Report	• Appointment of 'non-executive' directors. • Appointment of an audit committee to achieve greater control of financial reporting.
Greenbury Report	• Appointment of a remuneration committee to determine directors' remuneration and other pay issues. • Appointment of a nomination committee responsible for appointments to the board.
Hampel Report	• Largely consolidated recommendations of earlier reports into one 'Combined Code' (see below). • Improving communication with shareholders. • Redressing the balance between implementing controls and achieving business success by allowing companies discretion to apply corporate governance principles in the manner most suited to their organisation, and to explain deviations from 'best practice' to shareholders through their annual accounts.
Turnbull Report	• Giving directors, rather than operational managers, the responsibility for risk management and maintaining and reviewing a sound system of internal controls. • Basing internal control on a 'risk-based' approach. • Embedding such controls in the company's operations, with procedures for identifying and reporting control weaknesses so that appropriate remedial action can be taken.

Various recommendations have been made over the years aimed at improving the systems by which companies are directed and controlled including, most notably, those contained in the Cadbury Report, Greenbury Report, Hampel Report and Turnbull Report. Key recommendations put forward by these reports are summarised in the table above.

Whilst recommendations in these reports are essentially 'voluntary', meaning directors may exercise discretion over the manner and extent to which they adopt them, many of the best practice recommendations have been adopted by the UK Listing Authority and have been appended to the

Listing Rules in the form of the Combined Code, first issued in June 1998. This effectively means that directors of listed companies must adopt them and, if they do not, must explain why in a 'corporate governance statement' in their annual accounts (Listing Rule 12.43A and principles D1 and D2 of the Combined Code 1998).

More recently the Higgs Review was commissioned to review the role and effectiveness of non-executive directors and the adequacy of corporate governance arrangements to determine whether measures in the UK were sufficiently robust to prevent corporate failure and malpractice on the scale seen in the United States. At the same time, a review of the make up and responsibility of audit committees was being conducted by the FRC the results of which form the Smith Report.

The recommendations of the Higgs Review and the Smith Report have largely been included in the Combined Code 2003 issued by the FRC (to supersede and replace the 1998 Combined Code). The Combined Code 2003 applies to listed companies for reporting years beginning on or after 1 November 2003.

The Turnbull Report is important for determining the actual framework of a 'risk-based approach' to internal control and the Combined Code 2003 consolidates not only recommendations made in early reports on corporate governance but also those in the Higgs Review and the Smith Report.

The Turnbull Report and the Combined Code 2003 have been reproduced in Appendices 1 and 2. The main recommendations are summarised below.

i Turnbull Report

The Turnbull Report introduced the need for risk management within corporate governance and redefined internal control as the ongoing assessment and management of risks beyond those purely related to financial objectives and auditing.

As can be seen in Appendix 2, the report identifies the broad framework for internal control and risk management and requirements for the process by which controls are reviewed. It does not, however, prescribe any 'best' system, recognising that in reality this varies, depending on the company's culture, objectives, size, business environment, etc. and no one system would fit all companies. Such an approach encourages active consideration of internal controls and risk management by companies, rather than a box ticking exercise to satisfy regulatory requirements.

To the vast majority of companies, the need to manage and control risks will not be new as it has always been carried out (possibly in a more informal manner at an operational level) for companies to survive, overcome changes and keep ahead of competitors. What is possibly new is the need for the board to address, monitor and report on risk management and internal control.

Directors, especially those of listed companies, need to:

- determine formally the company's goals and objectives;
- identify what strategic, financial, compliance, contractual, physical, distribution, regulatory and other risks which would prevent the company achieving its goals;
- determine how to identify and measure these risks and the effects they are having on the company;
- establish a risk management structure through which to monitor performance;
- set up an internal system to manage and control risks to which the company may be or is exposed and review this internal system at least annually.

The Turnbull Report further recommends that the system of control be embedded in the company's operations and that it forms part of its culture. This certainly makes sense operationally as controls need to be integrated and understood throughout the company to ensure risks are identified, managed and mitigated at the earliest opportunity, minimising possible damage to the company or its performance.

ii Combined Code 2003

As can be seen in Appendix 1, the Combined Code 2003 contains main and supporting principles as well as provisions. Listed companies are required to make a disclosure statement in their annual report and accounts stating:

- how the company has applied the main and supporting principles; and
- that it has complied with the provisions of the Code and, where it has not, provided an explanation of the deviation.

Appendix 1 contains only the 'Code of Best Practice' from the Combined Code 2003 (the full text is available at www.frc.org.uk/publications/content/combined.pdf). The preamble makes it clear that, whilst listed companies are expected to comply the majority of the time, there will be exceptions and occasions where they do not.

Those evaluating compliance should take account of the company's size, complexity, challenges and risks and should not adopt a box-ticking approach to their review.

Whilst directors of listed companies will need to consult the text of the Combined Code 2003 in full, the main changes introduced by the Code's principles and provisions include recommendations that:

- at least half the board of a larger listed company be made up of non-executive directors;
- except in exceptional circumstances, the chief executive should not become the chairman and that the chairman be independent at the time of appointment;
- no individual be appointed as chairman of a second FTSE 100 company;
- a full-time executive director shall not take on more than one non-executive directorship in a FTSE 100 company, nor the chairmanship of such a company;
- once a non-executive director has served six years, his or her continued appointment be subject to a rigorous review and after nine years the non-executive would no longer be considered independent;
- a senior independent non-executive director be appointed and available to communicate with shareholders if required;
- the chairman should chair regular meetings of the non-executive directors but there should be at least one such meeting each year chaired by the senior non-executive director without the chairman present in order to assess his or her performance;
- the board should state in the annual report how a performance evaluation of the board, its committees and individual directors has been carried out;
- the board should establish an audit committee of at least three (or two for a smaller company) independent non-executive directors, at least one of whom has recent relevant financial experience; and
- the audit committee should monitor and review independence of the external auditors and, where they provide non-audit services, report in the annual report how objectivity and independence are safeguarded.

Performance Evaluation

Given that the purpose of the Combined Code 2003 is to improve the
effectiveness of the boards of listed companies, principles and provisions
have been included that set out requirements for information and professional development and evaluation of performance.

In the first instance, new directors should undergo formal induction
and thereafter continually update their skills and knowledge so that they
can fulfil their duties. The logic of these requirements is clear as induction
will help directors understand exactly what is required of them and, by
keeping up-to-date with changes in legislation and best practice, they will
continue to be able to make a valuable contribution as individuals and at
board and committee level.

The Code also requires the board to carry out a formal and rigorous
annual evaluation of its own performance and that of its committees and
individual directors. Detailed disclosure of how evaluation was carried
out is then required in the annual report. This reporting stage is
important as it focuses the chairman and board's attention on the need
for at least a yearly review and encourages the chairman to address
problems and take action where appropriate.

3   Length of service

There is nothing in the CA 1985 that limits the time a director may remain in office. The only restriction is that no one aged 70 or over can be appointed or remain a director of a public company or of a private company that is a subsidiary of a public company. This restriction can be waived by provisions in the company's Articles or by ordinary resolution of the members of which special notice has been given (CA 1985, s293).

A director may continue in office successfully for many years. However, this is not always the case; there may be circumstances where:

- the director decides to resign, for example because of time pressures, a parting of the ways with fellow directors who take no account of his or her views or opinions, or simply because another more attractive opportunity has emerged;
- the shareholders do not wish the director to continue in office, for example where they are concerned about the director's performance or motivation or the direction in which he or she is taking the company, and either seek to remove the director from office or not to reappoint him or her at the next AGM;
- there are specific restrictions in the company's Articles that prevent the director from continuing in office after, say, a given time or where the director ceases to be eligible and is required to vacate office.
- a non-executive director was appointed for a specified term, that period is up and a board review determines that re-election is not appropriate.

This chapter discusses:

- Resignation
- Removal
- Retirement by rotation
- Vacating office.

Resignation

Notwithstanding any restrictions in any contract of service, directors have the right to resign simply by tendering their resignation to the company (Table A, Reg 81(d)). Such resignation would normally need to be in writing and be addressed to the company's registered office.

The Articles usually require directors to give reasonable notice of their resignation but, in the absence of any such provision, a director can resign without the need for notice *(OBC Caspian Ltd v Thorp 1998 SLT 653, OH)*.

A director's resignation must be noted in the register of directors and notification be sent to Companies House, using prescribed Form 288b, within 14 days.

Removal

The members of a company may, at any time and notwithstanding anything in the company's Articles or any service contract with the director, remove a director from office by ordinary resolution approved in a general meeting of which special notice has been given (CA 1985, s303). Such removal is initiated when the company receives 'special notice' from a member detailing the member's intention to propose the resolution to remove a director at a general meeting.

Whilst the Articles cannot exclude this statutory right, they may permit removal by an alternative, and often simpler, means. For example, they may allow removal by majority vote of the other directors or merely by written notice from the holding company or the holder of the class of shares that appointed the director.

As removal of a director is a contentious matter and most often takes place when the relationship between the director and shareholders has irretrievably broken down, the remaining directors must ensure that the procedures set out in CA 1985 or those in the Articles are closely observed in order to avoid any recourse by the director so removed.

Retirement by rotation

Although there is no general requirement in CA 1985 for directors to retire by rotation at each AGM, such provision is usually included in the company's Articles (Table A, Regs 73 – 80). This provision serves to restore the balance of power between the shareholders and directors by giving the shareholders an opportunity to vote against a resolution to reappoint a particular director.

Prior to the AGM the directors will need to check the provisions on rotation in the company's Articles, as they vary tremendously. In many instances private and subsidiary companies, and those which have directors appointed by the holders of different classes of shares, exclude the need for retirement by rotation.

Table A requires all directors (except a managing director or director holding another executive office) to retire by rotation and offer themselves for re-election at the company's first AGM. Thereafter any directors appointed during the year must retire by rotation, together with one-third of the existing directors. In addition, the Combined Code requires that directors of fully listed companies offer themselves for re-election at least every three years.

Selection of which directors are due to retire by rotation will be based upon who has been longest in office since they were last reappointed. Where the director is willing to continue, wording of the resolution will be along the lines of *'That Mr XYZ, retiring by rotation in accordance with the Articles of Association, offers himself for reappointment as a director of the company'*. The resolution will be proposed as an ordinary resolution and be passed (or fail) on a simple majority.

Where the resolution for reappointment is approved, the director will continue in office. Where the resolution is not approved, the director will remain in office only until the end of the AGM, following which he or she will cease to be a director. This fact must be recorded in the register of directors and be notified to Companies House using prescribed Form 288b.

Vacating office

A company's Articles will usually provide that, when a person becomes prohibited from holding office as a director (see Chapter 1), the office of director shall be vacated.

The Articles may also specify other circumstances in which a director is required to vacate office, for example where the director:

- is, or may be suffering from mental disorder (Table A, Reg 81(c));
- fails to attend board meetings for six months without permission for absence (Table A, Reg 81(e));
- ceases to hold a shareholding qualification;
- has been in office for the maximum period specified in the Articles.

4   Origins of directors' duties

Statute does not set out an all-embracing code of conduct for directors, although such a proposal is under consideration as part of the Company Law Review. At present, directors need to have an understanding of what duties are imposed by common law and their contracts of service with the company, as well as by a considerable range of statutes.

This chapter covers:

- Duties embodied in common law
- Duties arising from service contracts.

Information on statutory duties is set out in following chapters.

Common law

It has long been established in common law that a director owes two types of duty to the company: a 'fiduciary duty' and a 'duty of skill and care'. Where a director breaches these duties, the company can take action to recover its property or to obtain payment of damages from the director as compensation for the loss incurred, and to recover any personal profit made by the director.

i   Fiduciary duty

The need for directors to observe their fiduciary duty to the company when contributing to and making decisions as part of the board means that directors must at all times:

- act in good faith and in the best interests of the company;
- use the powers conferred on them for the proper purpose;
- not put themselves in a position where they have an actual or potential conflict of interest with the company;
- not make any secret personal profit from opportunities that arise from their position as a director.

As can be seen from the above, these duties largely give rise to a negative obligation requiring directors *not* to do anything or make any decisions that conflict with the interests of the company.

The need for directors to observe their fiduciary duty is best illustrated by some sample cases.

CASE	DETAILS
Bhullar v Bhullar, Re Bhullar Bros Limited (2003) All ER (D) 445 (Mar)	One family which part-owned a limited company through which their grocery business was run became aware that property adjacent to the company's premises was for sale and bought it. The Court of Appeal held that the directors had breached their duty to communicate the availability of the property to the company and confirmed that it should be transferred to the company at purchase price.
British Midland Tools v Midland International Tooling [2003] All ER (D) 174 (Mar)	It was held that a number of directors had breached their fiduciary duties to the company where they knew a potential competitor was poaching the company's employees and did nothing to prevent it in the period prior to them joining the competitor.
Extrasure Travel Insurances Ltd v Scattergood [2003] 1 BCLC 598	Directors who transferred money from one group company to another merely to satisfy a pressing creditor had breached their fiduciary duties as it was not in the interests of the company to transfer the money. They were held liable accordingly.
JJ Harison (Properties) Ltd v Harrison [2001] 1 BCLC 158	A director used company resources to obtain planning permission on land which he bought from the company without informing his fellow directors of the planning status and without obtaining a market valuation. The director was held to have breached his duty to act in the best interests of the company and was required to account to the company for profits made.
Hogg v Cramphorn Ltd [1967] Ch 254	Directors who issued shares with enhanced voting rights to forestall a takeover bid, whilst they were acting in good faith, had breached their duty by making improper use of their powers to issue shares.

ii Duty of skill and care

Directors are required to exercise skill and reasonable care when acting in the company's interests.

Whilst traditionally (based on judgement in *City Equitable Fire Insurance Co Ltd [1925] Ch 407, CA*) the degree of skill required of a director was only that expected of an 'ordinary man' without need for him to be an expert, to possess any particular skills or to devote his continuous attention to the company's business, the requirements have been changing to take account of the fact that:

- many directors are full-time executives employed under contracts of service who are expected to bring particular skills and expertise to the company in exchange for sizeable remuneration;
- when determining whether a director should be personally liable for wrongful trading, the IA 1986, s214 applies a 'reasonable director' standard to determine what is expected of someone carrying out the director's function within the company.

As a consequence, more objective tests of the level of skill required of directors are being applied. This is illustrated in the recent case *Bairstow v Queens Moat Houses plc [2000] 1 BCLC 549* where the court held that an executive director is expected to bring to his work a level of competence commensurate with his responsibilities and for which he receives substantial remuneration.

In terms of the time and degree of attention a director is required to devote to the affairs of the company, there is a difference in what is expected from an executive director as opposed to a non-executive director. For non-executive directors, principles in *City Equitable* that directors are not required to give continuous attention to the affairs of the company and that their duties are intermittent can still be applied.

However, in contrast, executive directors will usually be required to devote their full time and attention to the business of the company, although the size and nature of the company will determine which matters receive personal attention.

Where the size of the company makes it impossible for directors to attend to all matters personally, delegation is permitted, provided there is adequate supervision (see Chapter 2). In *Re Barings plc; Secretary of State for Trade and Industry v Baker (1998) BCC 583*, when making a disqualification order the judge made it clear that, whilst directors may delegate functions, given the responsibilities of their office they must adequately supervise those carrying out the work even where they trust their competence and integrity. Furthermore, where directors seek professional advice, they must not rely solely upon the advice received without exercising their own judgement as they cannot absolve themselves entirely of responsibility by delegation *(Re Bradcrown Ltd [2001] 1 BCLC 547)*.

Service contracts

A director who has been appointed to an executive position would usually be provided with a service contract setting out not only individual rights relating to employment such as remuneration, holidays, entitlement to notice and other benefits, etc. but also duties to the company. These duties may be expressed in general terms, such as responsibility to:

- promote the interests of the company;
- carry out specific tasks as assigned by the board;
- devote time and attention to the company during agreed hours;
- observe all competition and confidentiality restrictions.

The contract may also contain specific and more detailed duties agreed between the director and the company relating to executive responsibilities of office, such as 'human resources'. In this instance the service contract may specify that the human resources director has responsibility for achieving specific staff turnover targets and responsibility for all personnel matters; ensuring that the company's employment practices and procedures are fully compliant with legislation and current recommendations for 'best practice'; data protection compliance; staff training, etc.

It is also important that provisions be included setting out the terms on termination. There has been considerable concern about large-scale severance payments made to directors of failing companies and the DTI is undertaking a review of severance pay and implementation of measures to ensure compensation reflects performance. In the meantime, careful contract negotiation and drafting is essential.

Requirements for approval of service contracts and disclosure requirements are dealt with in Chapter 7.

5   Disclosure requirements

There are a number of statutory duties arising from the CA 1985 that require directors to disclose certain information to the company, to the shareholders in the accounts, and to investigators appointed by the Secretary of State.

This chapter covers:

- Interest in contracts and transactions
- Interest in shares
- Investigations.

Interest in contracts and transactions

Directors must not put themselves in a position where there is a conflict between their personal interests and their fiduciary duty to the company. Similarly, directors cannot make a secret profit from a contract with the company (see Chapter 4).

To address this, under CA 1985, s317 a director who has any direct or indirect material interest in a contract or proposed contract, transaction or arrangement with the company must disclose this at a meeting of the directors. Provided disclosure has been made, the transaction is not voidable and the director will not be required to account for any benefit gained.

Failure to disclose such interest is a finable offence (CA 1985, s317(7)) and the director will in most instances be required to repay the company any personal profit made *(Regal (Hastings) Ltd v Gulliver [1942] 1 All ER 378)*.

It should also be noted that the board of directors has a corresponding duty to ensure that, when a director has disclosed an interest, it is recorded. Failure to do so exposes the company and every officer in default to a fine (CA 1985, s382(5)).

Disclosure must:

- be made by all directors of private and public companies, including 'shadow directors' (see Chapter 2) (CA 1985, s317(5));

- be made at the earliest opportunity;
- include the nature of the interest;
- be made at a meeting of the board of directors, not to a committee meeting *(Guinness plc v Saunders [1990] 2 AC 663)*, and it is not sufficient to record disclosure by resolution in writing (CA 1985, s317(1));
- be made and recorded in the minutes of the relevant board meeting even where the company has only a sole director *(Neptune (Vehicle Washing Equipment) Ltd v Fitzgerald [1995] 1 BCLC 352)*;
- be disclosed in the notes to the audited accounts (CA 1985, s232).

A director who is a member of another firm or company can disclose general notice of an interest without need for further disclosure at subsequent meetings.

Whilst the disclosure requirements of CA 1985, s317 cannot be abrogated by a company's Articles, the Articles can impose stricter requirements by, for example, prohibiting a director from being interested in any transaction with the company, although this is unusual (see Table A, Reg 85).

The Articles will usually state whether a director who has disclosed an interest can be counted in the quorum and vote on the matter under consideration (Table A, Reg 94). Rule 13.8 of the Listing Rules requires that the Articles of listed companies prohibit directors from voting on any contract, arrangement or proposal in which they have an interest except where it arises from holding shares or debentures of a listed company.

Interest in shares

Directors and shadow directors have a duty to disclose to the company their interest in shares and debentures of the company or of any holding or subsidiary company within the group structure (CA 1985, s324). A director who fails to make such disclosure, or makes a false disclosure statement will be guilty of an offence and be liable to imprisonment, a fine, or both.

Such disclosure must:

- be made in writing within five working days of the event that gave rise to the interest, such as an acquisition or, indeed, appointment as a director (CA 1985, ss324(1) and (2); Sch 13);
- include details of the number and class of shares or debentures in which the interest is held;

- include 'indirect interests' (CA 1985, Sch 13 Part I). This includes, for example, where the director is not the registered holder but has control over exercising the rights of the shares or debentures; the shares are held by a corporate body and the director controls at least one-third of its votes; the director has a joint holding; or where shares are held by the director's children or spouse (CA 1985, s328);
- be disclosed in the audited accounts, normally within the directors' report, giving a comparison between the interest at the beginning and end of the year (CA 1985, Sch 7 Part I) (see Chapter 9).

Appendix 3 gives a list of what should be included or excluded from disclosure.

The directors have a corresponding duty to record an interest notified by a director in the company's register of directors' interests (see Chapter 6) within three days of receiving the notification (CA 1985, s325). Furthermore, where the directors are aware that options to subscribe for shares or debentures have been granted to a director, they are required to note this in the register of directors' interests even where no formal notification is received.

In addition, where the director's disclosure of an interest concerns securities listed on the Stock Exchange, the company must announce the interest disclosed to the Regulatory Information Service, no later than the next business day following receipt of the notification (Listing Rule 16.4).

Investigations

The Secretary of State for Trade and Industry has power to investigate a company's affairs and membership and, where the company is subject to investigation, the company and all officers have a duty to co-operate with the investigation and to disclose such information as is required by the investigators (CA 1985, ss431–434).

There are many reasons for such investigations. For example, they may be initiated where it appears:

- the company's affairs have been conducted with intent to defraud creditors and others for a fraudulent, unlawful or prejudicial purpose (CA 1985, s432);
- that those involved in formation of the company or management of its affairs are guilty of fraud, misconduct or misfeasance towards the company or its members (CA 1985, s432);

- members have not been given all the information they might ordinarily be expected to receive (CA 1985, s432);
- there has been a contravention of restrictions on directors' dealing in share options of quoted securities (CA 1985, s323);
- the directors have failed to notify their interests in shares (CA 1985, s324);
- there is an apparent need to determine the people interested in shares or controlling the company;
- insider dealing has taken place, in contravention of CJA 1993, s52 and FSMA 2000.

The outcome of an investigation may lead to civil or criminal proceedings for a breach of duty or other statutory offences, a petition for the company to be compulsorily wound up, or a petition for relief by minority shareholders.

Once inspectors have been appointed, the company's directors, officers and agents have a duty to provide all assistance they could reasonably be expected to give to help the investigation. This includes disclosing and producing documents and attending before the inspectors when required to give evidence (CA 1985, s434(1)). Past and present officers may also be required to explain the content of documents provided (CA 1985, s447).

When an investigation is under way, it is an offence for directors to:

- fail to comply with a requisition to produce information or provide an explanation or statement of circumstances or to obstruct the inspector's right to search the premises, and they may be liable to a fine (CA 1985, s447(6)). Where they persistently fail to co-operate, directors may be held 'in contempt of court' and punishment will be at the discretion of the court (CA 1985, s436). For example, in *Re an inquiry into Mirror Group Newspapers plc [2000] Ch 194 [1999] All ER (D) 255*, a director who refused to co-operate was held 'in contempt of court' and was not entitled to refuse to answer questions;
- attempt to destroy, mutilate or falsify documents or make any false entries in any document or books of account. Where found guilty such a person will be liable to a fine, imprisonment, or both (CA 1985, s450);
- make a false statement or to provide a false explanation of events (CA 1985, s451).

6   Administrative duties

The general duties of directors contained in common law are augmented by an extensive range of specific duties imposed by statute. This chapter concentrates largely on administrative and compliance duties imposed by the CA 1985, including the directors' responsibility for:

- Appointing and removing officers
- Maintaining statutory records
- Filing requirements
- Retaining documents
- Displaying company details
- Paying dividends
- Political donations
- Bank accounts
- Paying tax
- Identifying money laundering
- Arranging insurance.

Whilst many of these are duties for which the company as a whole is responsible, the directors, by virtue of their position and the authority they hold as policymakers, are ultimately responsible for ensuring compliance. Even if the directors delegate responsibility to the company secretary (see Chapter 2), as is common practice, the directors remain ultimately responsible and in many instances will be liable with the company for contravention of statutory requirements. Furthermore, the directors may face disqualification for failing to fulfil these duties.

Appointing and removing officers

The directors have a duty to shareholders and others who have dealings with the company to ensure that officers required by statute are appointed. These include:

i Directors

Chapters 1 and 3 cover requirements in terms of the mechanics of appointment, resignation and removal. The directors must also ensure that any requirements for any minimum or maximum number of directors contained in the Articles are observed or risk the validity of their acts being called into question.

Where the number of directors falls below the minimum required by the Articles, the remaining directors do not have a right to continue to act unless specifically provided in the company's Articles (*Re Alma Spinning Co. (1880) 16 ChD 681*). Most Articles contain such a right, but in most instances it is limited to allowing the directors either to fill the vacancy themselves or to convene a general meeting for this purpose (Table A, Reg 90).

ii Auditors

Every company, except private companies exempt from the audit requirement and dormant companies exempt under CA 1985 s249AA, must appoint an auditor (CA 1985, s384, and see Chapter 9).

The directors have authority by CA 1985, ss385 and 388 to appoint the first auditor and to fill any casual vacancies. When appointing an auditor, they must ensure that the person or firm is properly qualified and eligible for appointment (CA 1989, ss25 and 30).

Furthermore, unless the company is private and has dispensed with the obligation to appoint auditors annually (CA 1985, s379A), the directors must ensure that the auditors' reappointment and remuneration are approved each year at the general meeting at which accounts are laid before the members (CA 1985, s386).

In January 2003 the Smith Report was published in response to a significant number of large-scale corporate collapses. Recommendations in the report, adopted in the Combined Code 2003, emphasised that the company's audit committee should monitor and review the performance of external auditors and the extent of their independence.

iii Company secretary

The directors must ensure there is a secretary of the company, and that the company secretary is not the same person as a sole director (CA 1985, s283). It is usual for the Articles to give authority to the directors to appoint and remove the company secretary (Table A, Reg 99).

The directors of a public company have a specific duty to ensure the person appointed has the requisite knowledge or qualifications to fulfil the position satisfactorily (CA 1985, s286). This is also important with private companies, as the person to whom the directors delegate many statutory duties must be capable of such tasks.

Maintaining statutory records

The directors are responsible for ensuring the statutory books and records of the company are kept up-to-date and are complete. Whilst this responsibility is a routine compliance matter, directors should give it as much attention as other matters. This was highlighted in *Re Bath Glass Limited (1987) 4 BCC 130*, where the decision to disqualify the director was in part for failure to maintain the register of directors. Failure to ensure compliance with these requirements will, in most instances, render the company, the directors and any officer in default liable to a fine.

Most statutory records need to be kept at the company's registered office (although there are exemptions, for example with the register of members and register of directors' interests). They comprise the following.

i Register of directors and secretaries

This register, containing details of current and past directors and secretaries, must be kept and be available for inspection by the company's shareholders or members of the public (CA 1985, 288).

ii Register of members

Every company must maintain a register containing details of members' names and addresses and the number of shares held (CA 1985, s352).

The directors must ensure that the register is available for inspection at the registered office or such other place as notified to Companies House, for example the offices of a share registration agent (CA 1985, s353). A copy of the register may be requested by members of the company or the general public and must be supplied within ten days of the request (CA 1985, s356).

iii Allotments and transfers

Whilst there is no statutory requirement to maintain such registers, it is both usual and good practice to keep them, to explain changes in the register of members and assist with completion of the annual return and disclosures to be made in the accounts each year.

iv Directors' interests

Every company must maintain a register containing the directors' interests in any shares or debentures of the company (CA 1985, s325). CA 1985, Schedule 13, Part IV requires the register to be available for inspection by members of the company or the general public, and a copy must be available for inspection at the AGM.

v Substantial interests

Public companies are required to keep a register in which any substantial interests disclosed by members are recorded within three days of the notification being received (CA 1985, s211). Notification should be made by a member:

- who acquires a 'material' interest of 3% or more, a 'non-material' interest of 10% or more, or a combination of the two amounting to 10% or more (e.g. 2% material + 8 % non-material), in the voting shares of the company; and
- where there is a change in that interest of 1% or more, or which takes the holding above or below the next percentage level (for example from 3.75% to 4.1%, or from 5.5% to 4.8%) (CA 1985, ss199(5)(b) and 200(1)).

This register must be available for inspection by members and others, and copies must be provided on request (CA 1985, s219). Furthermore, if the company has listed securities, information received about substantial interests must be notified to the Regulatory Information Service, in accordance with requirements of the Listing Rules, and be included in the company's accounts.

Where it appears that a member has acquired a notifiable interest without making the required disclosure, the directors of a public company must issue notice to that person to investigate the situation and determine who is the beneficial owner of those shares (CA 1985, s212).

vi Debenture holders

Whilst there is no statutory obligation to maintain a register containing details of debenture holders, it will help the directors keep accurate and reliable records. If such a register is maintained, it must be kept at the registered office (CA 1985, s190) and be available for inspection by members and the public.

vii Mortgages and charges

If there are fixed or floating charges, a register of mortgages and charges must be kept, together with a copy of every instrument creating the charge (CA 1985, s407). The register must be available for inspection by members, creditors and the public. If it is not made available, any officer in default will be liable to a fine (CA 1985, s408).

The directors have a corresponding duty to notify Companies House of the creation of a charge (CA 1985, s395). Failure to comply with the registration requirement will render the company and its officers liable to a fine.

viii Minute books

Every company is required to keep minutes of all general meetings, directors' meetings and meetings of managers (CA 1985, s382). The Articles would usually specify that minutes of committee meetings and holders of any class of shares must also be kept (Table A, Reg 100).

Minutes of general meetings would usually be kept separately from other minutes as they must be available for inspection by the members (CA 1985, s383) or members may request copies. Board minutes must be available for inspection by the auditors (CA 1985, s237) and the directors *(McCusker v McRae 1966 SC 253)*.

Filing requirements

As well as being responsible for maintaining the statutory books and records of the company, the directors have a corresponding duty to ensure that key changes in the company's location, structure and management are notified to Companies House on prescribed forms within specified periods. Most will be triggered by changes in the content or location of statutory records, for example:

- a change in registered office (CA 1985, s287);
- a change in directors or the secretary, or their details (CA 1985, s288);
- creation of a charge (CA 1985, s395);

- allotments of shares (CA 1985, s88(2));
- an increase in the authorised share capital (CA 1985, s123);
- consolidation, conversion or sub-division of shares (CA 1985, s122);
- purchase by a company of its own shares (CA 1985, s169);
- certain ordinary resolutions (such as removal of a director or auditor, or granting of authority to directors to allot shares);
- all special, extraordinary and elective resolutions (CA 1985, s380).

In each case the exact filing requirements and periods within which the forms must be submitted will differ. Appendix 4 includes further details about this and about other forms that must be submitted. Some forms can be submitted electronically, although at the moment this is quite limited (The Companies (Forms) (Amendment) Regulations 1998 and the Companies Act 1985 (Electronic Communications) Order 2000).

Failure to fulfil these filing requirements will render the directors and every officer in default liable to a fine and, for continued contravention, to a daily default fine.

Every company must also submit a signed annual return to Companies House within 28 days of the return date shown on the form, containing details of the company secretary, directors, shareholders, issued share capital, registered office, location of the registers of members and debenture holders and the company's principal business activity (CA 1985, s363, see also Appendix 5). Failure to comply is an offence for which the company, its directors and the secretary may be liable for prosecution. Whilst initial warnings will be issued to the company, letters will be sent to the directors warning them that criminal proceedings may be initiated against them for the default.

A copy of the company's annual report and accounts must also be submitted to Companies House, as described in Chapter 9.

Retaining documents

The volume of documents generated by most companies after a number of years trading means that it is not possible for them to retain all old files and records indefinitely due to limited storage space. In some instances off-site storage is either unavailable or unaffordable. Consequently directors must balance the need to reduce the volume of documents placed in storage with the need to ensure that documents are retained for as long as they may be required.

In making such assessment the directors must consider the following:
- 'Minimum retention periods' specified or implied in statute, which include:

  a) employment records – three years (Income Tax (Employment) Regulations 1993, Reg 55);

  b) documents relating to calculation of national insurance contributions – three years (Social Security (Contributions) Regulations 1979, as amended and Sch 1, para 32(5));

  c) VAT records where the company is registered for VAT – six years (Value Added Tax Act 1994, s58 and Sch 11, para 6(3)), although these records may be retained on microfilm, computer or other similar storage medium.

  As a general guide, documents relating to accounts, tax, VAT, personnel and employment details, share registration and health and safety matters have minimum retention periods. Directors must examine specific requirements before documents are destroyed and if there is a minimum retention period, must ensure documents are retained at least until this period has passed.

- The need for past records and documents to provide evidence in legal proceedings that the company discharged its duties satisfactorily. Directors should take care to ensure that documents are kept in the appropriate form until expiry of the period within which legal proceedings could be brought (the Limitation Act 1980, as amended). These include:

  a) product liability action within ten years of the date of supply;

  b) action for breach of contract within six years of the breach, unless the contract is under seal or executed as a deed, in which case it is 12 years;

  c) claims for personal injury within three years of the cause of the injury or when the plaintiff becomes aware of the injury;

  d) claims for negligence (other than those connected with (c) above), within three years of the damage or loss being discovered.

  Furthermore, whilst in most instances the courts accept copies of documents, such as microfilm or CD-ROM, as admissible evidence in legal proceedings (Civil Evidence Act 1968, s6), some civil and criminal proceedings may require original documents.

- Ongoing commercial and operational needs for the documents as a possible means of reference, etc.

- Retention periods implied or specified in the company's Articles. For example Table A, Reg 108 requires unpaid dividends to be held to a shareholder's account and repaid if claimed within 12 years of the date of declaration. Documents relating to dividends must be retained for at least this period.
- The possibility that the Inland Revenue might raise a tax assessment, which in normal circumstances can be at any time up to six years after the event (Taxes Management Act 1970, s34) or, where it suspects avoidance by fraud, wilful neglect or negligence has no time limit (Taxes Management Act 1970, ss 36 and 39).

Appendix 5 provides an indication of the statutory and recommended retention periods for documents, which may assist directors when considering whether to retain or dispose of records.

The directors could delegate responsibility for making this assessment to other people within the company provided they have a full understanding of the legal and commercial requirements for retaining documents. Once this process is complete, policies and procedures would usually be implemented to ensure that reasoned and informed decisions are made about which documents to retain and which to destroy or move into storage, on an ongoing basis.

Displaying company details

Every company is required to show the following information about the company clearly:

- Its name outside every office and premises in which business is carried on and outside the registered office (CA 1985, s348).
- The company name on all business letters, notices and official publications, order forms, endorsements, cheques and orders for money, receipts, invoices and credit notes (CA 1985, s349).
- The company's trading name (if applicable), place of registration, registered number and the address of the registered office (CA 1985, s351) on all business letters, order forms, invoices, receipts and payment demand notices. There are additional requirements if the company is a charity or investment company or wishes to show details of its directors or share capital on such documents.
- The correct company name on the company seal, if used (CA 1985, s350).

Failure to comply with these requirements will render the company and its officers liable to a fine. An officer of the company who signs a cheque or order for money which includes an error in the company's name, or uses a seal with an incorrect name, may be held personally liable *(Barber & Nicholls Ltd v R and G Associates (London) Ltd and Rogers [1981] CA Transcript 455, 132 NLJ 1076).*

Paying dividends

Directors generally have responsibility for a company's dividend policy. It is common practice for a company's Articles to authorise directors to declare and pay an 'interim' dividend, and to require that payment of a 'final' dividend recommended by the directors be approved by the members (Table A, Regs 102 and 103). Before a dividend is paid, the Articles' provisions must be checked, and any requirements for approval must be met.

Other requirements that directors must ensure are observed before a dividend is declared and paid include:

- the company's operational requirements, for example in terms of the need for re-investment of profits to fund expansion plans or the need to upgrade plant and machinery;
- observing preferential rights where shares of a particular class confer on the holders a preferential right to receive a dividend in preference to any other class of share;
- only paying the dividend where there are sufficient distributable profits (CA 1985, s263).

The directors must ensure 'relevant accounts' are prepared so that they can accurately determine the distributable profit available. These may comprise the last annual accounts, interim accounts or initial accounts where the company has not completed its first accounting period, subject to CA 1985, s270.

Directors who allow an 'illegal dividend' to be paid may be personally liable to repay the company (CA 1985, s277). In *Bairstow v Queens Moat Houses Plc [2002] BCC 91* the directors allowed a dividend to be paid out of capital; the court of appeal held that they were personally liable to repay £79 million to the company even where they were not recipients of the money.

Where the company's Articles permit, a dividend may be paid wholly or partly by the distribution of specific assets to shareholders, rather than by payment in cash (Table A, Reg 105).

Political donations

Under the Political Parties, Elections and Referendums Act 2000, before any political donations and expenditure associated with political parties (excluding membership fees) that exceed £5,000 are paid, they must be approved by the shareholders in general meeting (CA 1985, s347C). The payment cannot be ratified after the event and the directors may be required to repay the amount plus interest and any damages to the company (CA 1985, s347F).

Bank accounts

One of the first tasks the directors will have to undertake is to open a bank account in order that the company can make and receive payments when trading commences. The board must approve opening of the account and the terms and conditions by which the account is operated by the bank.

As part of their general duty to look after and protect the assets of the company, the directors must also give consideration to:

- suitable signatories and how to exercise adequate control of the account, for example by requiring a set number of signatures for payments above a certain monetary limit;
- frequency of bank statements;
- how often and by whom reconciliation of the bank account is carried out, for example monthly and by someone other than a signatory to the account, to keep the directors informed of the company's financial position;
- informing the bank of changes to the company's officers, especially where they are a signatory to the account and the bank mandate instruction needs to be revised.

Paying tax

Timely and accurate tax compliance is essential for any company, as severe financial penalties may be incurred where a company is late or inaccurate in making returns and interest may be charged on underpayments, which is obviously not the best use of a company's resources. The Inland Revenue's tax departments may also pursue criminal action against anyone guilty of tax evasion, or impose civil penalties for such offences (see Chapter 13).

Principal taxes include corporation tax, VAT, PAYE and national insurance. Whilst the task of computing and making required returns is usually delegated, the directors remain ultimately responsible for tax matters. They must therefore ensure that whoever carries out these day-to-day tasks is appropriately monitored to identify any irregularities or non-compliance at the earliest opportunity.

Identifying money laundering

Directors have a responsibility under POCA 2002 to implement procedures within the company to verify the identity of new clients and investors, etc. and to ensure adequate systems are in place for employees to identify and report any suspicion they may have that such client is involved in the laundering of illegally acquired funds.

POCA 2002 largely consolidates and updates money laundering offences in earlier legislation, it also extends the scope of offences to include:

- concealing, disguising, converting, transfering or removing criminal property;
- arranging or facilitating the acquisition or retention of criminal property; and
- acquiring, using or possessing criminal property.

As well as the better recognised money laundering offences, POCA 2002 extends to the proceeds of any crime and would include theft, tax evasion and burglary, etc.

Many companies address this responsibility by implementing a formal procedure to verify the identity of all new clients. For example, where transactions exceed a certain pre-determined amount or are always paid in cash, a company would usually require sight of an individual's passport and a utilities bill or, where the client is a company, carry out its own search of records at Companies House, check credit references and verify the identity of the company's principals in the same manner as for individual clients. Employees should be told who in the company is the 'money laundering reporting officer' to whom they should report any suspicions about clients, events or transactions.

Proposals are under consideration in the Money Laundering Regulations 2003 for a company's professional advisors, directors, secretary and others to be held personally liable for penalties where they should have known that money laundering was taking place.

Arranging insurance

Insurance policies form an important part of a company's risk management process by allowing a company to mitigate against potential financial loss when control measures implemented to avoid risks have failed. In general, directors should consider the following policies.

i Employer's liability insurance

This insurance must be effected by an employer, and failure to do so is a criminal offence. Typically the insurance will provide cover in respect of claims by employees for illness, bodily injury or disease caused during or arising as a result of their employment. The policy must provide for a minimum indemnity of £5 million on any single claim and be on display in the workplace. Old certificates of insurance need to be kept for 40 years.

ii Product liability insurance

Given the requirement that products must be safe for consumers to use, directors of a company that produces, supplies or imports products should obtain insurance to indemnify the company against the cost of a claim for damage caused by a defect in the product and the cost of having to withdraw or recall products from the market.

iii Directors' and officers' indemnity insurance

Directors can effect insurance against personal liability (CA 1985, s310(3)) which may arise when, for example, they have been negligent, made mistakes, committed a breach of duty, authority or trust, issued misleading statements or carried on wrongful trading. Such insurance may also cover the directors' costs incurred by investigation into their actions and those arising from disqualification proceedings. Directors, particularly of public companies, have much to gain from effecting such insurance to protect them against claims by shareholders, creditors, etc.

where, for example, they consider corporate failure was attributed to the directors' actions or they consider the directors' conflict of interest influenced the outcome of a merger or takeover. There are also considerable benefits to the company, as effecting such insurance may encourage the directors to have a more balanced attitude to risk, rather than always preferring the conservative, less risky approach. Indeed, the Combined Code 2003 recommends that a copy of this policy is provided to non-executive directors at the same time as their letter of appointment.

Recognising that choices over the type of insurance, extent of cover and exclusions can be confusing, ICSA have produced a guidance note on Directors' and Officers' Insurance to alert directors to some of the key issues when selecting a policy.

iv Employer's practices liability insurance

This is effected to provide cover against the cost of arbitration or tribunal proceedings, demands for compensation, punitive damages and defence costs should employment-related claims such as wrongful or unfair dismissal, direct or indirect discrimination, harassment and defamation be made against the company.

v Environmental insurance policy

It may be necessary to obtain a tailor-made environmental policy where the company's public liability policy does not extend to cover all pollution incidents which have been identified as a potential risk relevant to the company (for example 'gradual pollution' is often excluded).

Cover

Insurance policies' terms, conditions and exclusions vary tremendously and it is important the directors ensure the correct level of cover has been obtained. For example, in *Rexodan International Ltd v Commercial Union (Court of Appeal)* the company's product liability insurance only covered the cost of damaged products and not the cost of recall, loss of profits or packaging purchased that could not be used. This had disastrous financial implications for the company.

7   Restricted and prohibited transactions

There are a number of statutory duties arising from the CA 1985 restricting directors' actions, either by prohibiting certain acts or by requiring them to be approved in advance by the shareholders.

They include the following, which are covered in this chapter:

- Substantial property transactions
- Loans to directors
- Service contracts
- Takeovers and mergers.

Another prohibition is giving financial assistance with purchasing a company's shares, touched upon in Chapter 8.

Substantial property transactions

As a general rule a director of a company or of its holding company may not enter into an arrangement to acquire from or transfer to a company a 'non-cash asset' without first obtaining approval for the transaction from the members of the company by ordinary resolution in general meeting (CA 1985, s320(1)). This requirement extends to shadow directors and persons 'connected' with a director. It is largely concerned with preventing acquisitions at an inflated price and disposals at under their full value, that could arise due to a director's conflict of interest.

A 'material' transaction approved in accordance with CA 1985, s320 must be disclosed in the company's audited accounts.

Where the requirements of s320 are contravened and a transaction does not receive the necessary approval, the director or connected person and any other directors who authorised the transaction or arrangement will be liable to account to the company for any direct or indirect gain made from the transaction, or jointly to indemnify the company from any loss or damage arising from the transaction (CA 1985, s322(3)(a) and (b)).

For example, in *Re Duckwari plc [1997] Ch 201* a property was sold to a person connected to a director without shareholders' prior approval.

The connected person was required to pay the difference between the market value at the time of sale and the actual price paid. However, in other instances and within a reasonable time following the transaction, it may be possible for the members in general meeting to affirm or ratify what has taken place.

There are circumstances when shareholders' approval is not required, for example where:

- the asset is valued at less than £2,000;
- the asset is valued at less than £100,000 and comprises less than 10% of the company's net asset value;
- the arrangement is between a wholly-owned subsidiary and either the holding company or another wholly-owned subsidiary in the group;
- it is part of an arrangement where the company is being wound up (unless it is a members' voluntary winding-up (see Chapter 12));
- where the director is acquiring the asset in his or her capacity as a member of the company and not as a director, e.g. a distribution of assets rather than a payment of a cash dividend.

However, even where approval by the shareholders is not required, the director would be required to disclose his or her interest in the transaction to the board (see Chapter 5).

Loans to directors

To discourage directors from borrowing money from a company for their own benefit when it could be put to better use for the company, statutory obligations impose restrictions on loans to directors which they must ensure are observed. In general a company is not permitted to make a loan to a director, provide guarantee or security for any such loan, nor assume responsibility to a third party for a loan through a scheme of arrangement or assignment of liability by a director (CA 1985, s330).

The prohibition applies to shadow directors and directors of the holding company where a loan is proposed by a subsidiary, although a loan could be made by a holding company to a director of a subsidiary.

Where the company itself is a public company or has a public company within its group structure ('relevant company', CA 1985, s331(6)), the restrictions described above also apply to 'connected persons', and there are the following additional prohibitions:

All parties must avoid making any misleading statements that could create a false market in securities.

When an offer is received, directors of the offeree company must not take action to frustrate the offer without approval of the company's shareholders.

Minority interests must be protected.

The personal interests of directors of both companies must not influence any advice or recommendations they provide.

irectors must also ensure they do not deal in securities of either ·any when they have access to price-sensitive information.

gnising this, the shareholdings of directors and their dealings in the ·e and offeror companies in the 12 months leading up to the offer be disclosed.

ting Rules

isting Rules require that when a listed company is involved in a ver, an offer document in prescribed form and containing specific nation must be submitted to the UK Listing Authority for approval ng Rules 10.46 – 10.50).

here consideration for the takeover or merger consists of securities nich listing will be sought, it may be necessary to circulate listing ulars, or a summary thereof, to shareholders at the same time as the locument (Listing Rule 8.15).

- loans or quasi-loans (CA 1985, s330(3));
- credit transactions;
- provision of a guarantee or security for a loan, quasi-loan or credit transaction.

There are specific exemptions to this general prohibition in CA 1985 (set out in Appendix 6) which allow companies to make loans and enter credit transactions, etc. with directors. In each case the directors must ensure that the proposal is a permitted transaction and the qualifying criteria have been met before the transaction is authorised.

Where a loan is made in contravention of CA 1985, s330, any director who was involved in or authorised the transaction is guilty of an offence and is liable to the following civil and criminal sanctions:

- to account to the company for any direct or indirect gain made from the transaction and to indemnify it against any loss or damage suffered (CA 1985, s341);
- up to two years' imprisonment, a fine, or both (CA 1985, s342(1)).

The company may also demand immediate repayment of the loan *(Tait Consibee (Oxford) Ltd v Tait [1997] 2 BCLC 349, CA).*

Subject to a few exceptions, disclosure of transactions described in CA 1985, s330 must be made in the notes to the company's audited accounts and, where the company is part of a group, also in the group accounts (CA 1985, s232(1) and (2)). Furthermore, directors have a corresponding duty to notify the company of such matters that relate to them personally that need to be disclosed, and failure to do so is an offence (CA 1985, s232(3) and (4)).

Service contracts

Whilst generally a company's board of directors will have authority to negotiate the terms and conditions of a director's service contract without referring the matter to the members for approval, the following should be noted:

- the Articles may specify particular requirements for approval which must be observed, as failure to do so may result in the contract being unenforceable to the detriment of the company *(UK Safety Group Ltd v Heane [1998] 2 BCLC 208);*
- CA 1985, s319 requires that where a service contract is under consideration for a term of more than five years, the directors must

obtain prior approval of the members in general meeting. This
requirement also extends to:

- contracts for services such as consultancy agreements (CA 1985,
  s319(7));
- contracts which permit the director to extend the contract
  period to more than five years (ca 1985, s319(1));
- a contract for services of more than five years in a subsidiary
  company, in which case approval by members of both the
  subsidiary and the holding company is required.

Directors of listed companies also have to take into account corporate
governance requirements relating to service contracts, embodied largely
in recommendations of the Combined Code. These require that remuneration packages for executive directors are determined by the remuneration committee made up of non-executives and that notice periods on
service contracts be set at one year or less unless approved by the shareholders.

In addition to the requirements set out above, CA 1985, s318 and the
Listing Rules require that service contracts with more than 12 unexpired
months be made available for inspection by members as set out in
Appendix 7. Directors should be aware that any failure to make service
contracts available for inspection or to keep copies at the appropriate
location will expose the company and every officer in default liable to a
fine, plus a daily default fine where the contravention continues (CA 1985,
s318(8)).

Service contracts are also covered in Chapter 4.

Takeovers and mergers

In general, when considering or recommending an offer for a takeover or
merger, directors must observe their fiduciary duty to the company and
act honestly, in the best interests of both the company and the members as
a whole.

Where a director is to receive a payment, by way of compensation for
loss of office as a consequence of the proposal, details of the payment
(whether in cash or by the transfer of property) must be disclosed to, and
approved by, the members of the company (CA 1985, ss 312 and 313). In
addition, particulars of these payments must be disclosed in documents
sent to members (CA 1985, s314).

Failure by the directors, or any person properly instr
comply with these statutory requirements may lead to i
fine, and any unauthorised payment received by a direc
to be held 'on trust' for the members and may need to l
s315).

In addition, directors of listed companies must ensu
only requirements of the Listing Rules but also the Tak
below).

i Takeover Code

Issued by the Panel on Takeovers and Mergers, the Tal
out a number of general principles and rules governing
which takeovers and mergers of listed companies are c
not embodied in statute, failure to observe requiremer
Code can lead to disciplinary and other action by the
(such as private reprimand or public censure) or by th
regulatory body, such as the Financial Services Autho

Directors of the offeror and offeree company have
ensure that the requirements of the Code are compliec
conduct of an offer.

In addition to specific rules governing how and wh
the timing and content of announcements required, r
offeror and offeree company and the need to obtain a
competent independent advice to shareholders, etc.,
ensure the following general principles are observed:

- Members holding shares of the same class in th
  must be treated equally by the offeror.
- Information from the offeror and offeree must
  all shareholders.
- The offer should only be announced by the off
  directors are confident it can be implemented.
- Sufficient information must be supplied to sha
  them to make an informed decision.
- Reasonable time must be allowed for sharehol
  decision.
- High standards of care and accuracy must be
  mation supplied to shareholders.

8   Shareholders

It is fair to assume that the vast majority of shareholders are very reliant on the directors as they have only limited knowledge about what general meetings are required, how changes in share ownership occur, what decisions require shareholder approval and what information they should be sent by the company.

Directors therefore have an important role to play in managing the relationship between the company and its shareholders and in ensuring that restrictions and requirements in all shareholder matters are observed. To explain these responsibilities, this chapter covers:

- Share ownership
- General meetings
- Minority interests
- Communication.

Share ownership

Shareholders rely on directors to ensure that their rights are observed when any allotment, transfer, purchase or redemption of shares is being considered. Directors must make sure, before proceeding, that any requirements, restrictions or procedures governing such transactions as set out in the company's Articles and in statute are observed. A director who knowingly contravenes such requirements will be liable to civil liabilities and criminal penalties.

i   Allotment

The procedure for allotting shares is relatively straightforward, involving approval by the board and the issue of forms of application and acceptance. However, the directors must first check whether:

- the company has sufficient authorised but unissued shares from which to make the allotment and, where it does not, arrange for the authorised share capital to be increased by ordinary resolution approved by the members (CA1985,S121);

- the directors have the authority to allot shares, provided by the Articles or the members in general meeting (CA 1985, s80(1)). Where they do not, they can arrange for it to be provided by ordinary resolution of the members;
- shares must be offered pro rata to existing shareholders before being offered to other parties (CA 1985, s89 or by provisions in the company's Articles). Where there are such rights of 'pre-emption' and the proposal is for shares to be allotted other than pro rata to existing members, the directors must obtain:
  - individual consent to the allotment from each shareholder; or
  - approval from the members to a special resolution disapplying their statutory pre-emption rights (CA 1985, s95) or waiving the provisions in the company's Articles, whichever applies;
- any necessary shareholder qualification in the company's Articles is satisfied before a person can be admitted to membership;
- the allotment involves provision of financial assistance, which is generally unlawful (CA 1985, s151), although there are certain exceptions to this prohibition which may apply and should be checked (CA 1985, ss153 – 155). Where the directors permit shares to be acquired in circumstances where financial assistance is prohibited, they may be liable to a fine and imprisonment (CA 1985, s151(3));
- the allotment is for a public company and will involve offering shares to the public. If so, requirements of the Public Offers of Securities Regulations 1995, FSMA 2000 and the relevant market's rules may apply (for example, the Listing Rules for companies with securities quoted on the main Stock Exchange list) in addition to those of the CA 1985. In general these additional requirements relate to issue of offer documents and details required in the prospectus or listing particulars. The directors may be liable for civil and criminal penalties punishable by fine and/or imprisonment for making a false or misleading statement in the prospectus, and someone who has relied on this information may seek compensation from the directors (FSMA 2000, s90 and POS Reg 14);
- shares are to be allotted for cash or by way of a bonus or capitalisation issue, in which case provisions in the company's Articles must be observed and further approval of the shareholders is required. Shares may not be allotted at a discount (CA 1985, s100)

but may be allotted partly paid (observing the minimum requirements of CA 1985, s101 for a public company) and for consideration other than cash (observing CA 1985, ss103 and 108.)
Once all these initial requirements have been checked and complied with,
the directors may proceed with the allotment of shares, bearing in mind
their duty to ensure the allotment is in the best interests of the company
and not for any other purpose.

ii Transfer

Shares are essentially property and as such may freely be bought and sold
by members as provided in the company's Articles and in any shareholders' agreement (CA 1985, s182(1)). Directors are responsible
for maintaining the company's register of members (see Chapter 6)
and, as an extension of this duty, are responsible for registering share
transfers.

Whilst there may be additional provisions in a company's Articles,
registration of a transfer of shares would usually require approval of the
board. However, before such approval is given the directors must ensure:

- the stock transfer form submitted to them is appropriate (Table A,
  Reg 23), has been properly executed, and has either been signed on
  the reverse as 'exempt' from stamp duty or bears evidence that
  stamp duty has been paid;
- the transferor's share certificate is returned confirming ownership
  of the shares or, where this has been mislaid, a letter of indemnity is
  obtained from the transferor;
- any provisions or restrictions in the company's Articles (and any
  shareholders' agreement) are observed. For example, the Articles
  may contain pre-emption on transfer provisions requiring that any
  shares for sale are first offered to existing members in proportion to
  the number of shares they already own.

Once the requirements prescribed above have been complied with, the
directors may proceed to approve and register the transfer of shares.

It is worth noting that shares of public companies quoted on the main
Stock Exchange, AIM or OFEX must be freely transferable. In most
instances such companies' registers of members will be maintained by
share registration agents and the directors will only be aware of and
approve the transfers in batches when produced in reports for board
meetings.

iii Purchase and redemption

Provided there is authority in a company's Articles (Table A, Reg 3) every limited company with a share capital may issue redeemable shares (CA 1985,s159) and can purchase or redeem fully paid shares from the company's distributable profits or the proceeds of a new issue (CA 1985, s162) and, for private companies only, out of capital (CA 1985, s171).

It is important to note that where the Articles do not contain the necessary authority, the purchase of the shares is void under CA 1985, s143 and a court may order that the shareholder be restored to the register (*R W Peak (Kings Lynn) Ltd [1998] 1 BCLC 193*).

There are different requirements for redeeming and purchasing shares:

- 'Redeemable' shares must be redeemed in accordance with the provisions of redemption determined before, or at the time they were issued, set out either in the Articles or in a special resolution approved at that time. These requirements in terms of the date, terms and manner of redemption and price to be paid for the shares must be observed for the redemption to take place but they may, for example, merely require approval by the board at a specific time.
- Purchase by a company of its own shares is not usually a pre-planned or anticipated event, and a purchase contract, approved by special resolution of the members, is required before the purchase can proceed. This contract will determine the terms of the purchase (CA 1985, s164). Purchase can only take place where the company will be left with some non-redeemable shares in issue after the purchase. It can be paid for by a transfer of assets *(BDG Roof-Bond Ltd v Douglas [2000] 1 BCLC 401)*.

Where the purchase or redemption is to be financed out of capital, there are additional tight statutory controls to protect creditors' interests, as a reduction of capital reduces funds available to creditors should the company be wound up. Directors therefore have a duty to ensure the following additional requirements are observed:

- The directors must make a statutory declaration that the company will continue as a 'going concern' for at least a year after the payment from capital has been made (CA 1985, s173). It is an offence for the directors to make such declaration without reasonable grounds, punishable by up to two years' imprisonment.

The directors may also be personally liable to creditors where the company is wound up within a year of the redemption or purchase out of capital (IA 1986, S76 (2)(b)).

- Payment out of capital, as well as the purchase contract, must be approved by special resolution of the members.
- Payment out of capital can only be made when distributable profits and the proceeds of any new issue of shares have been exhausted (S171(3)).
- No capital can be applied to pay a premium on the shares.
- 'Relevant accounts' must have been drawn up, together with a report from the auditors confirming the directors' calculation of the permissible capital payment (CA 1985, S172(3)) and there must be nothing unreasonable stated in the directors' declaration (CA 1985, S173(5)).
- A notice about the purchase must appear in the London Gazette and either be published in a national newspaper or notified individually to all creditors (CA 1985, S175(2)).

Finally, should the purchase or redemption involve listed securities, the directors must also consult requirements for obtaining approval and making announcements in the relevant market's listing rules and ensure they are observed. Directors of listed companies should be aware that from 1 December 2003, The Companies (Acquisition of Own Shares) (Treasury Shares) Regulations 2003 (SI 2003/1116) amend CA 1985 S162 and introduce new sections 162 A–G to allow listed companies to hold qualifying shares bought back by the company in treasury. This means the shares can be held ready for resale at a later date.

General meetings

Directors have a duty to ensure that no decisions are made or actions taken on matters outside their authority. They must be aware of the limits of their authority and of the circumstances where members' approval must be sought in general meeting.

General meetings are meetings of the company's members. However, it is extremely unlikely that the members will be aware of requirements governing how such meetings are convened and held so they will rely heavily on the directors.

In practice, responsibility for ensuring all procedural requirements for general meetings are met is usually delegated to the company secretary (see Chapter 2). However, the board retains ultimate responsibility for general meetings and it is important the directors are at least aware of the basic requirements, as set out below.

i Convening the meeting

A company's Articles normally provide the directors with power to convene general meetings as and when required, and the board would normally hold its own meeting to discuss the matter and authorise the secretary or a director to issue notice of the meeting to members. In addition, CA 1985, s377 states that the directors are responsible for convening an annual general meeting (AGM) each year and, should they fail to do so, they will be liable to a fine (CA 1985, s366(4)).

The directors should also be aware that the shareholders may:

- convene an extraordinary general meeting (EGM) at any time by requisition in writing deposited at the company's registered office (CA 1985, s368);
- requisition the directors to include particular resolutions in the notice of a general meeting or to circulate a statement with the notice (CA 1985, s376).

In both instances, once the directors have checked and determined the validity of the requisition, they must comply with its requirements within the relevant time.

ii Types of meeting

The most frequent members' meetings are AGMs and EGMs. However, where different classes of share have been issued, it may also be necessary to convene a class meeting where the resolutions would vary the rights of a class of shares (CA 1985, s125).

AGM

A company must hold one AGM each year within 15 months of the previous year's (CA 1985, s366) unless the company either is a private company and has passed a special resolution to dispense with this requirement (CA 1985, s366A) or is newly incorporated, in which case the first AGM must be held within 18 months of incorporation regardless of the calendar year.

The Articles usually determine what routine business must be considered at the AGM, such as re-appointment of directors (Table A, Reg 73), receipt of the annual accounts, approval of any final dividend and re-appointment of the auditors. Public companies would also normally routinely include renewal of the directors' authority to allot shares and waiver of pre-emption rights on allotment of shares. Other 'special business' can be considered at the AGM where the timing is such that it can be included in the notice of the meeting.

EGM

As only one AGM can be held each year, all other general meetings held in the year are called EGMs. Such meetings are held where approval by members is required for a particular matter and timing is such that it cannot wait until the next AGM.

There are also a few instances where the CA 1985 specifically requires a matter to be considered at an EGM, for example a public company reporting a serious loss of capital (CA 1985, s142). The business to be conducted at the EGM will be set out in the notice.

Class meetings

Where resolutions to be proposed at an AGM or EGM include proposals to reorganise a company's share capital, change entitlement to dividends, alter voting rights or wind up the company, etc. and there is more than one class of share in issue, separate meetings of the holders of the classes of shares may be necessary. Requirements for class meetings are contained in CA 1985, s125 as well as the company's Articles and any shareholders' agreement.

It should also be noted that, except where the resolutions proposed are to remove a director or an auditor, on most other occasions members of private companies may approve resolutions in writing as an alternative to holding a general meeting (CA 1985, s381A) and members of public companies may approve resolutions in writing where such authority is specifically included in the company's Articles (Table A, Reg 53). The written resolution procedure is a very valuable alternative where a company has a small number of shareholders, a decision is required quickly and the directors are confident all shareholders will agree the proposals, as unanimous consent is required.

iii Notice of meeting

The directors, usually with assistance from the company secretary, are responsible for formulating and sending notice of general meetings and class meetings to members. They must ensure that all members who have a right to attend and vote at such meetings are sent the notice either by post or email, or by display on a website (provided members have been notified of the latter).

Directors have a duty to ensure:

- the notice is correct and complies with statutory requirements as well as provisions in the company's Articles. For example, Table A, Reg 38 requires the notice to state the meeting's date, time and location and the general nature of business to be conducted; CA 1985, s366(1) requires an AGM to be specified as such; CA 1985, s372(3) requires details about the right to appoint a proxy to be included. The authority under which the notice is issued must be shown, and further notes about inspection of documents and 'cut-off' dates for members on the register may be required for companies with shares listed on the main Stock Exchange market, AIM or OFEX.
- the type of resolution proposed in the notice is correct. This is essential, to ensure the resolution is not invalidated by failure to give sufficient notice or to secure the required percentage of votes for the resolution to be passed. Such resolutions may be ordinary, extraordinary, special or elective. Requirements for notice and votes required as well as a description of circumstances where they may be required is contained in Appendix 8.
- the length of notice given is sufficient in accordance with the statutory requirements shown below, and taking account of any longer period that may be required by provisions in the company's Articles.

TYPE OF MEETING	LENGTH OF NOTICE
AGM	21 days (CA 1985, s369(1))
EGM	14 days (CA 1985, s369(1))
EGM (to consider a special resolution)	21 days (CA 1985, s378(2))
General meeting of an unlimited company	7 days (CA 1985, s369(2)(B))
Class meeting	14 days (CA 1985, s125(6))

- loans or quasi-loans (CA 1985, s330(3));
- credit transactions;
- provision of a guarantee or security for a loan, quasi-loan or credit transaction.

There are specific exemptions to this general prohibition in CA 1985 (set out in Appendix 6) which allow companies to make loans and enter credit transactions, etc. with directors. In each case the directors must ensure that the proposal is a permitted transaction and the qualifying criteria have been met before the transaction is authorised.

Where a loan is made in contravention of CA 1985, s330, any director who was involved in or authorised the transaction is guilty of an offence and is liable to the following civil and criminal sanctions:

- to account to the company for any direct or indirect gain made from the transaction and to indemnify it against any loss or damage suffered (CA 1985, s341);
- up to two years' imprisonment, a fine, or both (CA 1985, s342(1)).

The company may also demand immediate repayment of the loan *(Tait Consibee (Oxford) Ltd v Tait [1997] 2 BCLC 349, CA)*.

Subject to a few exceptions, disclosure of transactions described in CA 1985, s330 must be made in the notes to the company's audited accounts and, where the company is part of a group, also in the group accounts (CA 1985, s232(1) and (2)). Furthermore, directors have a corresponding duty to notify the company of such matters that relate to them personally that need to be disclosed, and failure to do so is an offence (CA 1985, s232(3) and (4)).

Service contracts

Whilst generally a company's board of directors will have authority to negotiate the terms and conditions of a director's service contract without referring the matter to the members for approval, the following should be noted:

- the Articles may specify particular requirements for approval which must be observed, as failure to do so may result in the contract being unenforceable to the detriment of the company *(UK Safety Group Ltd v Heane [1998] 2 BCLC 208)*;
- CA 1985, s319 requires that where a service contract is under consideration for a term of more than five years, the directors must

obtain prior approval of the members in general meeting. This requirement also extends to:

- contracts for services such as consultancy agreements (CA 1985, s319(7));
- contracts which permit the director to extend the contract period to more than five years (ca 1985, s319(1));
- a contract for services of more than five years in a subsidiary company, in which case approval by members of both the subsidiary and the holding company is required.

Directors of listed companies also have to take into account corporate governance requirements relating to service contracts, embodied largely in recommendations of the Combined Code. These require that remuneration packages for executive directors are determined by the remuneration committee made up of non-executives and that notice periods on service contracts be set at one year or less unless approved by the shareholders.

In addition to the requirements set out above, CA 1985, s318 and the Listing Rules require that service contracts with more than 12 unexpired months be made available for inspection by members as set out in Appendix 7. Directors should be aware that any failure to make service contracts available for inspection or to keep copies at the appropriate location will expose the company and every officer in default liable to a fine, plus a daily default fine where the contravention continues (CA 1985, s318(8)).

Service contracts are also covered in Chapter 4.

Takeovers and mergers

In general, when considering or recommending an offer for a takeover or merger, directors must observe their fiduciary duty to the company and act honestly, in the best interests of both the company and the members as a whole.

Where a director is to receive a payment, by way of compensation for loss of office as a consequence of the proposal, details of the payment (whether in cash or by the transfer of property) must be disclosed to, and approved by, the members of the company (CA 1985, ss 312 and 313). In addition, particulars of these payments must be disclosed in documents sent to members (CA 1985, s314).

Failure by the directors, or any person properly instructed by them, to comply with these statutory requirements may lead to imposition of a fine, and any unauthorised payment received by a director will be deemed to be held 'on trust' for the members and may need to be repaid (CA 1985, s315).

In addition, directors of listed companies must ensure they observe not only requirements of the Listing Rules but also the Takeover Code (see below).

i Takeover Code

Issued by the Panel on Takeovers and Mergers, the Takeover Code sets out a number of general principles and rules governing the manner in which takeovers and mergers of listed companies are conducted. Whilst not embodied in statute, failure to observe requirements of the Takeover Code can lead to disciplinary and other action by the Takeover Panel (such as private reprimand or public censure) or by the relevant regulatory body, such as the Financial Services Authority.

Directors of the offeror and offeree company have a responsibility to ensure that the requirements of the Code are complied with in the conduct of an offer.

In addition to specific rules governing how and when an offer is made, the timing and content of announcements required, responsibilities of the offeror and offeree company and the need to obtain and communicate competent independent advice to shareholders, etc., the directors must ensure the following general principles are observed:

- Members holding shares of the same class in the offeree company must be treated equally by the offeror.
- Information from the offeror and offeree must be made available to all shareholders.
- The offer should only be announced by the offeror when its directors are confident it can be implemented.
- Sufficient information must be supplied to shareholders to allow them to make an informed decision.
- Reasonable time must be allowed for shareholders to make a decision.
- High standards of care and accuracy must be applied to all information supplied to shareholders.

- All parties must avoid making any misleading statements that could create a false market in securities.
- When an offer is received, directors of the offeree company must not take action to frustrate the offer without approval of the company's shareholders.
- Minority interests must be protected.
- The personal interests of directors of both companies must not influence any advice or recommendations they provide.

The directors must also ensure they do not deal in securities of either company when they have access to price-sensitive information. Recognising this, the shareholdings of directors and their dealings in the offeree and offeror companies in the 12 months leading up to the offer must be disclosed.

ii Listing Rules

The Listing Rules require that when a listed company is involved in a takeover, an offer document in prescribed form and containing specific information must be submitted to the UK Listing Authority for approval (Listing Rules 10.46 – 10.50).

Where consideration for the takeover or merger consists of securities for which listing will be sought, it may be necessary to circulate listing particulars, or a summary thereof, to shareholders at the same time as the offer document (Listing Rule 8.15).

8   Shareholders

It is fair to assume that the vast majority of shareholders are very reliant on the directors as they have only limited knowledge about what general meetings are required, how changes in share ownership occur, what decisions require shareholder approval and what information they should be sent by the company.

Directors therefore have an important role to play in managing the relationship between the company and its shareholders and in ensuring that restrictions and requirements in all shareholder matters are observed. To explain these responsibilities, this chapter covers:

- Share ownership
- General meetings
- Minority interests
- Communication.

Share ownership

Shareholders rely on directors to ensure that their rights are observed when any allotment, transfer, purchase or redemption of shares is being considered. Directors must make sure, before proceeding, that any requirements, restrictions or procedures governing such transactions as set out in the company's Articles and in statute are observed. A director who knowingly contravenes such requirements will be liable to civil liabilities and criminal penalties.

i   Allotment

The procedure for allotting shares is relatively straightforward, involving approval by the board and the issue of forms of application and acceptance. However, the directors must first check whether:

- the company has sufficient authorised but unissued shares from which to make the allotment and, where it does not, arrange for the authorised share capital to be increased by ordinary resolution approved by the members (CA1985,s121);

- the directors have the authority to allot shares, provided by the Articles or the members in general meeting (CA 1985, s80(1)). Where they do not, they can arrange for it to be provided by ordinary resolution of the members;
- shares must be offered pro rata to existing shareholders before being offered to other parties (CA 1985, s89 or by provisions in the company's Articles). Where there are such rights of 'pre-emption' and the proposal is for shares to be allotted other than pro rata to existing members, the directors must obtain:
  - individual consent to the allotment from each shareholder; or
  - approval from the members to a special resolution disapplying their statutory pre-emption rights (CA 1985, s95) or waiving the provisions in the company's Articles, whichever applies;
- any necessary shareholder qualification in the company's Articles is satisfied before a person can be admitted to membership;
- the allotment involves provision of financial assistance, which is generally unlawful (CA 1985, s151), although there are certain exceptions to this prohibition which may apply and should be checked (CA 1985, ss153 – 155). Where the directors permit shares to be acquired in circumstances where financial assistance is prohibited, they may be liable to a fine and imprisonment (CA 1985, s151(3));
- the allotment is for a public company and will involve offering shares to the public. If so, requirements of the Public Offers of Securities Regulations 1995, FSMA 2000 and the relevant market's rules may apply (for example, the Listing Rules for companies with securities quoted on the main Stock Exchange list) in addition to those of the CA 1985. In general these additional requirements relate to issue of offer documents and details required in the prospectus or listing particulars. The directors may be liable for civil and criminal penalties punishable by fine and/or imprisonment for making a false or misleading statement in the prospectus, and someone who has relied on this information may seek compensation from the directors (FSMA 2000, s90 and POS Reg 14);
- shares are to be allotted for cash or by way of a bonus or capitalisation issue, in which case provisions in the company's Articles must be observed and further approval of the shareholders is required. Shares may not be allotted at a discount (CA 1985, s100)

but may be allotted partly paid (observing the minimum requirements of CA 1985, s101 for a public company) and for consideration other than cash (observing CA 1985, ss103 and 108.)

Once all these initial requirements have been checked and complied with, the directors may proceed with the allotment of shares, bearing in mind their duty to ensure the allotment is in the best interests of the company and not for any other purpose.

ii Transfer

Shares are essentially property and as such may freely be bought and sold by members as provided in the company's Articles and in any shareholders' agreement (CA 1985, s182(1)). Directors are responsible for maintaining the company's register of members (see Chapter 6) and, as an extension of this duty, are responsible for registering share transfers.

Whilst there may be additional provisions in a company's Articles, registration of a transfer of shares would usually require approval of the board. However, before such approval is given the directors must ensure:

- the stock transfer form submitted to them is appropriate (Table A, Reg 23), has been properly executed, and has either been signed on the reverse as 'exempt' from stamp duty or bears evidence that stamp duty has been paid;
- the transferor's share certificate is returned confirming ownership of the shares or, where this has been mislaid, a letter of indemnity is obtained from the transferor;
- any provisions or restrictions in the company's Articles (and any shareholders' agreement) are observed. For example, the Articles may contain pre-emption on transfer provisions requiring that any shares for sale are first offered to existing members in proportion to the number of shares they already own.

Once the requirements prescribed above have been complied with, the directors may proceed to approve and register the transfer of shares.

It is worth noting that shares of public companies quoted on the main Stock Exchange, AIM or OFEX must be freely transferable. In most instances such companies' registers of members will be maintained by share registration agents and the directors will only be aware of and approve the transfers in batches when produced in reports for board meetings.

iii Purchase and redemption

Provided there is authority in a company's Articles (Table A, Reg 3) every limited company with a share capital may issue redeemable shares (CA 1985,s159) and can purchase or redeem fully paid shares from the company's distributable profits or the proceeds of a new issue (CA 1985, s162) and, for private companies only, out of capital (CA 1985, s171).

It is important to note that where the Articles do not contain the necessary authority, the purchase of the shares is void under CA 1985, s143 and a court may order that the shareholder be restored to the register (*R W Peak (Kings Lynn) Ltd [1998] 1 BCLC 193*).

There are different requirements for redeeming and purchasing shares:

- 'Redeemable' shares must be redeemed in accordance with the provisions of redemption determined before, or at the time they were issued, set out either in the Articles or in a special resolution approved at that time. These requirements in terms of the date, terms and manner of redemption and price to be paid for the shares must be observed for the redemption to take place but they may, for example, merely require approval by the board at a specific time.

- Purchase by a company of its own shares is not usually a pre-planned or anticipated event, and a purchase contract, approved by special resolution of the members, is required before the purchase can proceed. This contract will determine the terms of the purchase (CA 1985, s164). Purchase can only take place where the company will be left with some non-redeemable shares in issue after the purchase. It can be paid for by a transfer of assets *(BDG Roof-Bond Ltd v Douglas [2000] 1 BCLC 401)*.

Where the purchase or redemption is to be financed out of capital, there are additional tight statutory controls to protect creditors' interests, as a reduction of capital reduces funds available to creditors should the company be wound up. Directors therefore have a duty to ensure the following additional requirements are observed:

- The directors must make a statutory declaration that the company will continue as a 'going concern' for at least a year after the payment from capital has been made (CA 1985, s173). It is an offence for the directors to make such declaration without reasonable grounds, punishable by up to two years' imprisonment.

The directors may also be personally liable to creditors where the company is wound up within a year of the redemption or purchase out of capital (IA 1986, S76 (2)(b)).

- Payment out of capital, as well as the purchase contract, must be approved by special resolution of the members.
- Payment out of capital can only be made when distributable profits and the proceeds of any new issue of shares have been exhausted (S171(3)).
- No capital can be applied to pay a premium on the shares.
- 'Relevant accounts' must have been drawn up, together with a report from the auditors confirming the directors' calculation of the permissible capital payment (CA 1985, S172(3)) and there must be nothing unreasonable stated in the directors' declaration (CA 1985, S173(5)).
- A notice about the purchase must appear in the London Gazette and either be published in a national newspaper or notified individually to all creditors (CA 1985, S175(2)).

Finally, should the purchase or redemption involve listed securities, the directors must also consult requirements for obtaining approval and making announcements in the relevant market's listing rules and ensure they are observed. Directors of listed companies should be aware that from 1 December 2003, The Companies (Acquisition of Own Shares) (Treasury Shares) Regulations 2003 (SI 2003/1116) amend CA 1985 S162 and introduce new sections 162 A–G to allow listed companies to hold qualifying shares bought back by the company in treasury. This means the shares can be held ready for resale at a later date.

General meetings

Directors have a duty to ensure that no decisions are made or actions taken on matters outside their authority. They must be aware of the limits of their authority and of the circumstances where members' approval must be sought in general meeting.

General meetings are meetings of the company's members. However, it is extremely unlikely that the members will be aware of requirements governing how such meetings are convened and held so they will rely heavily on the directors.

In practice, responsibility for ensuring all procedural requirements for general meetings are met is usually delegated to the company secretary (see Chapter 2). However, the board retains ultimate responsibility for general meetings and it is important the directors are at least aware of the basic requirements, as set out below.

i Convening the meeting

A company's Articles normally provide the directors with power to convene general meetings as and when required, and the board would normally hold its own meeting to discuss the matter and authorise the secretary or a director to issue notice of the meeting to members. In addition, CA 1985, s377 states that the directors are responsible for convening an annual general meeting (AGM) each year and, should they fail to do so, they will be liable to a fine (CA 1985, s366(4)).

The directors should also be aware that the shareholders may:

- convene an extraordinary general meeting (EGM) at any time by requisition in writing deposited at the company's registered office (CA 1985, s368);
- requisition the directors to include particular resolutions in the notice of a general meeting or to circulate a statement with the notice (CA 1985, s376).

In both instances, once the directors have checked and determined the validity of the requisition, they must comply with its requirements within the relevant time.

ii Types of meeting

The most frequent members' meetings are AGMs and EGMs. However, where different classes of share have been issued, it may also be necessary to convene a class meeting where the resolutions would vary the rights of a class of shares (CA 1985, s125).

AGM

A company must hold one AGM each year within 15 months of the previous year's (CA 1985, s366) unless the company either is a private company and has passed a special resolution to dispense with this requirement (CA 1985, s366A) or is newly incorporated, in which case the first AGM must be held within 18 months of incorporation regardless of the calendar year.

The Articles usually determine what routine business must be considered at the AGM, such as re-appointment of directors (Table A, Reg 73), receipt of the annual accounts, approval of any final dividend and re-appointment of the auditors. Public companies would also normally routinely include renewal of the directors' authority to allot shares and waiver of pre-emption rights on allotment of shares. Other 'special business' can be considered at the AGM where the timing is such that it can be included in the notice of the meeting.

EGM

As only one AGM can be held each year, all other general meetings held in the year are called EGMs. Such meetings are held where approval by members is required for a particular matter and timing is such that it cannot wait until the next AGM.

There are also a few instances where the CA 1985 specifically requires a matter to be considered at an EGM, for example a public company reporting a serious loss of capital (CA 1985, s142). The business to be conducted at the EGM will be set out in the notice.

Class meetings

Where resolutions to be proposed at an AGM or EGM include proposals to reorganise a company's share capital, change entitlement to dividends, alter voting rights or wind up the company, etc. and there is more than one class of share in issue, separate meetings of the holders of the classes of shares may be necessary. Requirements for class meetings are contained in CA 1985, s125 as well as the company's Articles and any shareholders' agreement.

It should also be noted that, except where the resolutions proposed are to remove a director or an auditor, on most other occasions members of private companies may approve resolutions in writing as an alternative to holding a general meeting (CA 1985, s381A) and members of public companies may approve resolutions in writing where such authority is specifically included in the company's Articles (Table A, Reg 53). The written resolution procedure is a very valuable alternative where a company has a small number of shareholders, a decision is required quickly and the directors are confident all shareholders will agree the proposals, as unanimous consent is required.

iii Notice of meeting

The directors, usually with assistance from the company secretary, are responsible for formulating and sending notice of general meetings and class meetings to members. They must ensure that all members who have a right to attend and vote at such meetings are sent the notice either by post or email, or by display on a website (provided members have been notified of the latter).

Directors have a duty to ensure:

- the notice is correct and complies with statutory requirements as well as provisions in the company's Articles. For example, Table A, Reg 38 requires the notice to state the meeting's date, time and location and the general nature of business to be conducted; CA 1985, s366(1) requires an AGM to be specified as such; CA 1985, s372(3) requires details about the right to appoint a proxy to be included. The authority under which the notice is issued must be shown, and further notes about inspection of documents and 'cut-off' dates for members on the register may be required for companies with shares listed on the main Stock Exchange market, AIM or OFEX.

- the type of resolution proposed in the notice is correct. This is essential, to ensure the resolution is not invalidated by failure to give sufficient notice or to secure the required percentage of votes for the resolution to be passed. Such resolutions may be ordinary, extraordinary, special or elective. Requirements for notice and votes required as well as a description of circumstances where they may be required is contained in Appendix 8.

- the length of notice given is sufficient in accordance with the statutory requirements shown below, and taking account of any longer period that may be required by provisions in the company's Articles.

TYPE OF MEETING	LENGTH OF NOTICE
AGM	21 days (CA 1985, s369(1))
EGM	14 days (CA 1985, s369(1))
EGM (to consider a special resolution)	21 days (CA 1985, s378(2))
General meeting of an unlimited company	7 days (CA 1985, s369(2)(B))
Class meeting	14 days (CA 1985, s125(6))

Listed companies must also adhere to the Combined Code's requirement that notice be sent to shareholders at least 20 working days before the AGM.

The Articles usually also specify the number of days required for notice as 'clear days', i.e. they usually exclude the day of posting and day of the meeting and allow one or two days for postal delivery.

Members can agree a shorter notice period (CA 1985, S369) where the need for urgent business decisions makes it necessary for the directors to convene and hold a general meeting or class meeting with less than the required period of notice. Such agreement must be obtained from members in the percentages set out below.

TYPE OF MEETING	NUMBER OF MEMBERS REQUIRED TO AGREE TO SHORT NOTICE
AGM	All members entitled to attend and vote (CA 1985, S369(3))
Other general meetings	Members holding not less than 95% of shares having the right to vote (CA 1985, S369(4))*
Meeting where a special resolution is proposed	Members holding not less than 95% of shares having the right to vote (CA 1985, S378(2))*
Class meeting	Members holding not less than 95% of the relevant class of shares having the right to vote (CA 1985, S369)

*Note: where the company is a private company, this percentage may be reduced to 90% by elective resolution to that effect (CA 1985, S369(4) and 378(3)).

In practical terms, the directors can only take advantage of these provisions where the company has a relatively small number of members as, although the Act does not specify it as a requirement, it is essential for evidential purposes that agreement to a meeting being held on short notice is obtained in writing. The directors must check the signed agreements to ensure that the necessary percentage approval has been obtained before they proceed and hold the general or class meeting. Failure to do this may invalidate the proceedings conducted at the meeting.

iv Holding the meeting

The directors' role of advising shareholders continues while general meetings and class meetings are being conducted. This is principally fulfilled by the chair and company secretary, assisted by the other directors.

Together they need to ensure that business is conducted in a manner that complies with requirements in the company's Articles and any relevant statutory provisions, so that the validity of the meeting and resolutions passed cannot be questioned.

ICSA's publication *A Guide to Best Practice for Annual General Meetings* and guidance notes *Polls – Chairman's Obligations* and *Proxy Instructions – Abstentions* provide more detailed information about these particular aspects of the meeting. Suffice here to say that the directors will need to check provisions relating to the following:

- **Chair** – the Articles usually state that this shall be the chair of the board or in the chair's absence another director (Table A, Reg 42). However, there may be other provisions requiring election of a chair.

- **Quorum** – the meeting cannot proceed to business until the quorum, usually stated in the Articles, is present. If the Articles do not state a quorum, CA 1985, ss370 and 370A require two members to be present personally, unless there is only one member of the company, in which case a sole member shall be a quorum.

- **Voting** – shareholders' voting rights and the manner in which voting shall be conducted will be specified in the company's Articles and should be established before the meeting. For example:
  - holders of different classes of shares may have different rights to vote;
  - the vote may be conducted by show of hands or on a poll: the Articles will specify who can call a poll and how it is to be carried out;
  - 'best practice' requires the chair to call a poll where the chair knows proxy votes received will, on a poll, give a different result to the show of hands;
  - where the company has shares listed on the main market of the Stock Exchange, the Combined Code (as well as PIRC, NAPF and other shareholder action groups) requires the chair to announce

what proxy votes have been received on each resolution, even where the resolution is approved on a show of hands.

- **Proxies** – the directors must check to ensure who at the meeting has been appointed a proxy to attend and vote on behalf of a member (CA 1985, s372). This is important as, unless the Articles provide otherwise, a proxy is not entitled to vote on a show of hands and may be restricted from speaking at the meeting (CA 1985, s372(2)(c)).
- **Corporate representatives** – companies such as institutional investors are entitled to appoint a 'corporate representative' to attend general meetings and vote on their behalf (CA 1985, s375). Although a number of investor bodies consider this area to be in need of reform, as the law stands only one representative is permitted to represent each corporation and the directors must ensure that this restriction is observed.

v Minutes and resolutions

Once the meeting has been held, the directors must ensure that minutes recording business conducted are prepared, signed and placed in the company's minute book (CA 1985, s382). These signed minutes are evidence of matters approved at the meeting and must be retained. In addition, where certain types of ordinary resolutions and all special and extraordinary resolutions are approved, signed copies of the resolutions will need to be submitted to Companies House, for which the directors will be responsible.

Minority interests

General meetings are an important part of the company process whereby shareholders with the right to vote are involved in decision making. However, directors must be aware that, whilst the general principle is that decisions are made by approval of the majority of members, where the directors themselves hold and control the majority of votes, they have a duty not to abuse their position.

Directors must ensure that they strike a balance in their recommendations and the need to protect minority shareholders' interests. For example, a recommendation to pay large and unjustified directors' bonuses may be considered unjust and detrimental to minority shareholders who are not also directors.

A member (or members) who considers the company's affairs to have been conducted in an unfairly prejudicial manner has a number of remedies available including:

- applying to the Secretary of State for an investigation of the company's affairs (CA 1985, s431);
- petitioning the court for a 'just and equitable' winding-up in situations where the management of a company has broken down or opposing parties have reached an irresolvable deadlock (LA 1986, s122(1)(g));
- applying to the court for an order on the basis that the company's affairs have been conducted in such a way as to be 'unfairly prejudicial' to members generally or some part of them (CA 1985, s459). The order may result in the court regulating the future conduct of the company's affairs; instructing that the act or omission considered prejudicial be stopped or carried out; a person being authorised to take civil proceedings for a wrongdoing in the name of the company; or the member's shares being repurchased by the company or other members (CA 1985, s461(2)(d)).

For example, in *Re Brenfield Squash Racquets Club Ltd [1996] 2 BCLC 184* the majority shareholder caused the company to enter into arrangements, including giving a bank guarantee, which had no benefit to the company and was to the detriment of the minority shareholder. The court held that appropriate relief for the minority shareholder was the sale of shares by the majority shareholder to the minority shareholder in accordance with the pre-emption clause in the company's shareholders' agreement.

Directors should also note that, even where a company genuinely needs additional funds to be raised by a rights issue, a minority shareholder unable to participate in the rights issue may be able to restrain the issue on the basis that his or her interest would be diluted *(Hall v Gamut Technologies Ltd 1999 SLT 1276, OH)*.

Communication

An important principle for directors to remember is that they have been appointed by the shareholders to operate and manage the company on their behalf. It is therefore in the directors' own interests to establish good relations with shareholders who, in effect, have control of their future.

Directors are accountable to shareholders for progress of the company and have a duty to report to them on its performance.

Company law and the UK Listing Authority's regulations require that directors automatically send certain information to shareholders, such as the annual report and accounts, interim statements (listed companies only), and notice and details of any resolutions to be proposed in general meeting. This will ensure that shareholders are kept informed about the financial status and the company's progress and are aware of any proposed decisions that require their approval. In addition to this, the Higgs Review has recommended that a senior independent director be identified and available to communicate with shareholders should they have any concerns. It is proposed that this recommendation be included in requirements of the Combined Code (see Appendix 1).

The Companies Act 1985, (Electronic Communications) Order 2000 allows a company to send necessary documents to a shareholder's nominated electronic address, to permit the company to place company information on a website accessible to members, and to accept proxies sent by email. Many companies have found that an increasing number of shareholders are signing up to electronic communications. Directors would be well advised to consult ICSA's publication *Electronic Communications with Shareholders – ICSA's Guide to Recommended Best Practice.*

Many company directors recognise the value of good shareholder relations and have established shareholder communication policies which extend beyond the limits of 'compulsory' information required to be sent to shareholders by the UK Listing Authority and statute. Such policies are supported and recommended as 'best practice' by ICSA. This additional communication may take the form of:

- a timely response to all shareholder enquiries by the management executive best able to provide an answer;
- supplying quarterly financial reports;
- sending circulars to shareholders on plans, current developments, etc.;
- ensuring that market information and reports reach the financial press;
- holding briefing meetings with institutional investors and analysts;
- making information on the company's progress and development available through the internet and establishing this as a two-way channel of communication.

At the same time, many company directors have expanded the business conducted at the AGM beyond statutory requirements as they recognise the value of this meeting, not only for compliance, but also as a forum through which they can communicate details of the company's performance over the past year. Holding the AGM is an expensive and time consuming business, which can be put to best use by:

- explaining items of business in the notice of the meeting clearly and minimising use of confusing legal terms;
- ensuring that accounts are not 'laid' before the meeting as a purely symbolic act, but are made part of the business of the meeting and fully discussed;
- encouraging constructive questions;
- giving oral, video or graphic presentations and reports on items such as the company's performance, market information and opportunities, new strategies and technological developments, either before or as part of the meeting, which will help to widen the shareholders' understanding of the company as a whole;
- providing information in an appropriate form to specialist share-holder groups, for example by the use of braille in printed documents, audio tapes or large print.

Although the directors' duty to impart this additional information is not embodied in statute, as their appointment is secured by the members and a vote to confirm re-appointment of some directors is usually part of the business at each AGM, many would consider establishing good relations with shareholders to be vital. Indeed, the value and importance of the AGM as a means of communicating with shareholders forms an integral part of corporate governance recommendations, and it is likely that there will be improvements, certainly amongst listed companies, both in the amount and means by which information is imparted to shareholders.

However, following enactment of the FSMA 2000, which took effect on 1 December 2001, directors need to exercise a certain amount of caution, together with advance planning to ensure that communication with shareholders of a listed company, whether at the AGM, in writing or otherwise, does not amount to 'market abuse' which is an offence under s118, FMSA 2000. The FSA's Code of Market Conduct sets out three broad types of behaviour that amount to market abuse:

- **Misuse of information** – behaviour based on information not generally available and which is relevant to an investor's dealings in an investment. This offence is similar to the existing offence of insider dealing and may occur, for example, following dissemination of information at an AGM that has not been previously or simultaneously disclosed or announced.

- **Creating a false or misleading impression** – behaviour likely to give a false or misleading impression about the price, value, supply or demand of an investment. Directors therefore need to ensure that all information they convey, whether verbally, in writing or via internet bulletin boards and chat sites, etc. is completely accurate and does not mislead the recipient.
- **Distorting the market** – behaviour that manipulates the market value of an investment by interfering with the normal process of supply and demand.

More details about the standards required can be found in the FSA's Code of Market Conduct (see www.fsa.gov.uk). Directors should be aware that they could face unlimited financial penalties, be ordered to pay compensation to persons affected and be publicly censured for any breach.

It is therefore very important to ensure that no price-sensitive information is inadvertently communicated at the AGM without having been announced at or before the meeting. It is recommended that directors give advance consideration to likely questions and appropriate answers.

9 Financial accounts

Directors must ensure detailed and comprehensive accounting records are maintained to fulfil their role as managers and custodians of a company's assets and to ensure they are aware of the company's true financial position at any given time and are able to make more informed decisions. They must also ensure that annual accounts are prepared and submitted to Companies House and presented to the shareholders for adoption.

To explain these duties further, this chapter covers:

- Accounting records
- Preparation of accounts
- Reports required
- Notes to the accounts
- Approval of accounts
- Laying and delivering accounts
- Accounting exemptions
- Audit exemptions
- Additional requirements for listed companies.

Accounting records

The directors are responsible for maintaining detailed accounting records so that, at any time, they are able to demonstrate and explain the company's financial position and determine what transactions have taken place (CA 1985, s221). More specifically, directors have a duty to:

- keep accounting records which are sufficient to record and explain transactions and provide a reasonably accurate picture of the financial position of the company at any time;
- provide information from which to compile the balance sheet and profit and loss account for the annual accounts;
- keep records of all money received and paid out on a daily basis;
- maintain records of assets and liabilities;
- where applicable, carry out a year-end stock take and keep records of stock levels;

- where goods are sold other than in the normal course of retail business, to keep details of the buyers and sellers so that they can be identified.

Failure to maintain adequate accounting records will cause every officer in default to be liable to a fine, imprisonment, or both (CA 1985, s221(5) and (6)).

The accounting records must be kept at the company's registered office or such other place as the directors consider appropriate and must be open for inspection by the company's officers at any time. They must be retained for a minimum statutory period of three years for a private company and six years for a public company. An officer found guilty of failing to take sufficient measures to ensure accounting records are retained or of acting deliberately to defraud will be liable to a fine, imprisonment, or both (CA 1985, s222(6)).

In most instances the directors delegate responsibility for maintaining accounts to one executive director, usually called the 'finance director', who has the required accounting knowledge and experience to fulfil this function. Such a director will usually be responsible for managing the day-to-day accounting function, and for compiling detailed accounting information and reports, such as monthly management accounts, cashflow statements, profit projections, forecasts and budgets for consideration by the board. The quality of the information provided is paramount, as it often forms the basis of key strategy decisions on how to manage and deploy the company's resources to best effect.

Preparation of accounts

CA 1985, s226 requires the directors to prepare a profit and loss account for each financial year of the company, together with a balance sheet made up to the last day of that year. The provisions of CA 1985, Sch 4 prescribe in detail the form and content of the accounts and set out five basic accounting principles which must be applied when preparing the accounts:

- **Going concern** – as long as it is applicable, the company must be treated as if it will continue business and operations on the same scale for the foreseeable future.
- **Consistency** – accounting policies must be applied consistently from one financial year to the next to allow comparisons to be made.

- **Prudence** – the value of any item in the accounts must be determined on a 'prudent basis' by taking account of actual profit realised before the end of the financial year and any liabilities or losses that have arisen or are likely to arise in that period.
- **Accruals** – any income and charges must be taken into account in the financial period to which they relate, without regard to when they are paid or received.
- The value of **assets or liabilities** in the balance sheet must be individually determined.

Directors should also be aware that additional provisions may apply, for example where the company is a banking or insurance company (CA 1985, s255) or where it is part of a group that requires consolidated accounts for the group (CA 1985, s227).

The finance director will usually draft the annual accounts in close association with the company's auditors to ensure the form and content is correct and relevant accounting standards and principles have been applied. Any departure from the prescribed format, or any change in the format used from one year to the next, can only be made where the directors consider there are special reasons for the change and they explain this in the notes to the accounts.

Reports required

As well as a profit and loss account and balance sheet, the accounts must include a directors' report and an auditors' report (CA 1985, ss234 and 235). In addition a directors' remuneration report is required for a quoted company (CA 1985, s234B) and the government is also consulting on proposals for an 'operating and finanical review' (OFR) for inclusion in quoted companies' annual reports.

i Directors' report

The directors' report accompanying the accounts must include the information required by CA 1985, s234 as well as Sch 7 which, in brief, includes the following:

- a fair review of the business of the company (and subsidiaries) during the year and the position at the end of the year;
- the amount of any dividend recommended by the directors;
- names of directors who held office during the year;*

- the principal activities of the company (and subsidiaries) during the year and any significant changes;*
- substantial differences between market value of land and the value stated in the balance sheet where the directors consider they need to be brought to the attention of members or debenture holders;
- details of directors' interests in the shares of the company at the beginning and end of the year and details of share options held by them and whether any options were exercised during the year;*
- political and charitable contributions which exceed £200;*
- important post-balance sheet events for the company (and subsidiaries);
- mention of any likely future developments for the company (and subsidiaries);
- details of research and development by the company (and subsidiaries);
- particulars of any acquisitions of own shares during the year;*
- details of any branches of the company outside the UK;
- where the average number of employees exceeds 250 during the year:
  - the company's policy on employing disabled people;
  - a statement of employee involvement, including details of communication, procedures for consulting employees and arrangements to encourage involvement in the company's performance, such as an employee share scheme;
- where the company is a public company or subsidiary of a public company, its policy on payment of trade creditors.

Where the directors fail to prepare a directors' report, or the contents do not comply with the requirements set out above, all directors who were in office immediately before the period for laying and delivering accounts shall be guilty of an offence and liable to a fine (CA 1985, s234(5)).

Only those items marked with an asterisk (*) need to be included in the directors' report of a small company.

ii Statement of directors' responsibilities

Directors are required by the Statement of Accounting Standards, Auditors' Reports on Financial Statements (SAS 600) to comply with the Cadbury Report's recommendation to include a directors' responsibility statement in the annual accounts. Such reports must detail the directors' responsibility to:

- prepare accounts that give a true and fair review of the company's state of affairs;
- select suitable accounting policies and apply them consistently;
- make judgements and estimates that are prudent and reasonable;
- state whether applicable accounting standards have been followed, subject to any material departures disclosed and explained in the notes;
- prepare accounts on a going concern basis unless it is not appropriate (where there is no separate Going Concern Statement in the accounts (see page 79));
- maintain proper accounting records, safeguard the company's assets and take reasonable steps to prevent and detect fraud or other irregularities.

iii Auditors' report

Unless specifically exempt from the obligation to appoint auditors (see page 76), the accounts must include a report from the auditors confirming whether, in their opinion:

- the balance sheet, profit and loss account and any group accounts give a true and fair view of the state of affairs of the company and profit and loss for the year;
- the accounts have been properly prepared (CA 1985, s235).

The directors must ensure the auditors have access to all books and records they require to audit the accounts fully and are provided with any information and answers to questions they raise. Should this not be the case, the auditors have a specific duty to disclose this fact in their report to the accounts (CA 1985, s237).

Whilst the auditors' report in the accounts submitted to Companies House must bear the original signature of the auditors and state their name, copies sent to members and others entitled to receive them can merely state the name of the auditors (CA 1985, s236).

It should also be noted that, to provide shareholders with more detailed information, many companies, especially those which are listed, include additional information. For example, the annual report and accounts will often contain a statement from the chair providing an overview of performance and prospects for the company and may also contain detailed reports and information on environmental and health and safety performance, etc.

iv Directors' remuneration report

Directors of a quoted company must prepare a directors' remuneration report to accompany the accounts. This report must include the information set out in Sch 7A which, in brief, requires details of:

- the names of directors on the remuneration committee and consultants who advised on remuneration;
- the company's policy on remuneration including a summary of performance conditions attaching to options and incentive plans, explanation of why these criteria were selected and how performance is measured, details of any external comparison figures required and of any changes in entitlement. If there are no performance conditions this needs to be explained, as does the importance of the performance-linked elements of the remuneration package;
- each element of individual director's remuneration packages, set out in a table, including basic salary and fees, bonuses, expenses allowance, benefits in kind, compensation for loss of office or early termination and any other non-cash benefits;
- the company's policy on granting options or awards under its employee share schemes or other long-term incentive schemes and explanation of any deviation from policy;
- each director's share options set out in a table;
- long-term incentive schemes and each director's interest at the beginning and end of the accounting period, with details of grants or commitments made;
- any element of remuneration, other than basic salary, which is pensionable;
- director's service contracts including the date, unexpired term, notice period and compensation payable on early termination;
- any contributions paid for each director pursuant to any defined benefit scheme or money purchase scheme;
- the aggregate of excess retirement benefits paid to directors, past directors, their dependents or nominees;
- significant payments to former directors made during the year;
- consideration paid to third parties for the services of any director;

- share price performance, in the form of a graph, compared to comparitor companies with an explanation of why comparitors have been chosen.

Where directors fail to prepare a directors' remuneration report, or the contents do not comply with the requirements set out above, all directors who were in office immediately before the period for laying and delivering accounts shall be guilty of an offence and liable to a fine (CA 1985, S234B(3)).

v Operating and financial review ('OFR')

Whilst at present the inclusion of an OFR in a company's annual report is voluntary, many companies do include reviews which contain important information about the company's current position and prospects for the future. The need for an OFR is endorsed by the Accounting Standards Board and in January 2003 the ASB issued a revised statement setting out their recommendations on the content of the OFR (available at www.asb.org.uk). Furthermore, the ICAEW has issued guidance to assist directors when gathering information and conducting the OFR entitled: *Preparing an Operating Financial Review: Interim Process Guidance for Directors.*

In addition the Government has put forward proposals in the White Paper 'Modernising Company Law' for an OFR to be included in every major company's annual report. If the proposals are accepted and enacted, compliance will be obligatory and the OFR would include:

- a statement about the company's business for the year;
- a projection of prospects and description of events which could substantively effect prospects; and
- an explanation of community, social, environmental and employment issues of relevance to the company's business.

Whilst many companies already include OFRs in their annual reports, proposals that the OFR be the responsibility of the board and that a formal process be put in place to prepare the OFR mean that there is still much work to be done.

Notes to the accounts

Certain information must be set out in the notes to the accounts, which is explained below. However, the notes also contain other information necessary to support and explain calculations and information shown elsewhere in the accounts.

Any director, or past director who ceased to be a director less than five years previously, has a duty to inform the company of personal information which must be disclosed in the notes to the accounts, and to ensure that the required disclosures are made (CA 1985, S232).

CA 1985, Sch 6 (as amended by the Company Accounts (Disclosure of Directors' Emoluments) Regulations 1997, SI 1997/570) requires disclosure of the following information in the notes to the accounts, unless there is a specific reason for exemption:

- the aggregate amount of directors' emoluments (excluding company contributions to pension schemes);
- the aggregate amount of gains made on exercise of share options;
- the aggregate amount of money or other assets (excluding share options) paid to or received by directors under long-term incentive schemes;
- pensions of past and present directors (including entitlement to emoluments waived) and sums paid to third parties for directors' services;
- any loans, quasi-loans or other dealings in favour of directors or connected persons and details of any agreements to enter into such arrangements or agreements;
- any transactions, arrangements and agreements made by the company, or any subsidiary company, with officers of the company other than directors;
- compensation paid to directors for loss of office, which now includes payments in respect of breach of directors' contracts.

CA 1985, Sch 5 also requires details of 'related undertakings' (being parent or subsidiary companies in which at least a 10% interest is held) to be disclosed in the notes to the accounts.

Failure by directors to make the required disclosures should come to light during the audit and, if not rectified, must be reported in the auditors' statement to the accounts (CA 1985, S237).

Approval of accounts

When the accounts have been finalised, they must be approved by the board of directors and:

- the balance sheet must be signed by a director on behalf of the board (CA 1985, S233);
- the directors' report must be signed by either a director or the company secretary (CA 1985, S234A).

The copy of the accounts submitted to Companies House must bear original signatures, whilst copies sent to members and others entitled to receive accounts must include the names of the signatories. Failure to comply with these requirements will render the company and any officer guilty of an offence and liable to a fine.

Laying and delivering accounts

All company directors have a duty to lay the accounts before the members and to deliver a signed copy to Companies House within specific time periods, as discussed below. It is a criminal offence for the directors to fail to do so and it is important for directors to note that even where a company has been dissolved and Companies House decides not to prosecute, a private prosecution could be brought by, for example, a creditor, and the directors could be fined and ordered to pay costs for their failure to file accounts.

i   Laying accounts before members

The directors have a duty to lay the annual report and accounts before the company in general meeting (CA 1985, S241), unless the company is a private company and has passed an elective resolution dispensing with this requirement (CA 1985, S379A). Whilst this would normally be carried out at the AGM, accounts may be laid before the members at any general meeting convened for the purpose.

When convening the meeting and sending out copies of the annual report and accounts, directors should be aware that:

- copies of the company's annual accounts, the directors' report, (for a quoted company) the directors' remuneration report and the auditors report which are usually all bound into one document commonly referred to as the 'annual report and accounts' must all be laid before the company in general meeting (CA 1985, S241(1)).
- the general meeting must be convened with the appropriate period of notice, unless consent to a shorter notice period is approved by the members (see Chapter 8);

- every member, debenture holder and person entitled to receive notice of the general meeting must be sent a copy of the annual report and accounts (either by post or by electronic means) at least 21 days before the general meeting at which they are to be laid before the members (CA 1985, s238(1)), although they may waive this requirement in favour of a shorter period (CA 1985, s238(4));
- whilst a small or medium-sized company (see page 75) may be permitted to submit 'abbreviated' or 'modified' accounts to Companies House, the directors must ensure that full accounts are circulated to members and laid before them at the general meeting;
- where the company is a listed public company and has circulated a 'summary financial statement' to members, the full annual report and accounts must be laid before the members at the general meeting;
- unless the company has elected otherwise, the dormant accounts must be sent to members and others entitled to receive copies and be laid before the company in general meeting;
- even where the members have passed an elective resolution to dispense with the requirement to hold an AGM each year, they must still be sent a copy of the annual report and accounts once approved by the directors, together with a notice informing them of their right to require the directors to convene a general meeting to lay the accounts and reports before the members if they so require (CA 1985, s253).

ii Delivering accounts to Companies House

The directors of every company, even where the company is dormant or has ceased trading, have a statutory duty to prepare and submit the annual report and accounts to Companies House within the periods set out below (CA 1985, ss242 and 244):

- **Private company** – ten months from the end of the accounting period.
- **Public company** – seven months from the end of the accounting period.
- **New private company** – 22 months from the date of incorporation, or three months from the end of the accounting reference period (whichever is later).
- **New public company** – 19 months from the date of incorporation, or three months from the end of the accounting reference period (whichever is later).

In some instances these periods can be extended by making application to the Secretary of State. This could be where there are extenuating circumstances such as the need to finalise a legal issue that has an important bearing on the accounts, which cannot be finalised until the outcome is known, or where there is a delay because the company carries on business or has interests outside the UK, Channel Islands or Isle of Man (CA 1985, ss244(3) and (5)). In both cases the application must be made before expiry of the period in which accounts are required to be filed.

Where the directors fail to ensure that the accounts are delivered to Companies House within the required period, they will be guilty of an offence and liable to a fine (CA 1985, s242(1)). In addition, the company is subject to a civil penalty, which falls due when the overdue accounts are submitted and is calculated as follows (CA 1985, s242A):

NUMBER OF MONTHS LATE	PUBLIC COMPANY	PRIVATE COMPANY
Up to three	£500	£100
More than three but less than six	£1,000	£250
More than six but less than twelve	£2,000	£500
More than 12	£5,000	£1,000

Where the accounts are not submitted within the required period, Companies House will notify the directors of their responsibility and, if no response is received, will commence legal proceedings against the directors and the company.

Directors should note that the accounts submitted to Companies House must be printed in black type or ink on good quality A4 white paper, have a matt finish, bear original signatures and not have shaded areas or photographs. If these requirements are not met, Companies House will reject the accounts as they cannot be easily microfilmed and scanned onto its image database.

Accounting exemptions

Subject to satisfying qualifying criteria set out below, 'small' or 'medium-sized' private companies and groups may qualify for exemptions in preparation of their accounts (CA 1985, ss246, 246A, 247A, 247B and 248A), as will a company which is 'dormant'.

To qualify for small or medium-sized company or group exemptions (discussed below), the company or group must satisfy at least two of the following criteria (CA 1985, s247):

	SMALL COMPANY £	MEDIUM-SIZED COMPANY £
Turnover not more than ...	2.8m	11.2m
Balance sheet total not more than ...	1.4m	5.6m
No of employees (monthly average) not more than ...	50	250

However, the special provisions and exemptions discussed below do not apply to public companies, banking or insurance companies, authorised persons under FSA 1986, or members of an ineligible group (containing any one of these), even if the company satisfies the above criteria.

i Small companies

A small company does not have to deliver a profit and loss account, directors' report or full balance sheet to Companies House. It may instead submit abbreviated accounts comprising a modified balance sheet prepared in accordance with CA 1985, Sch 8A, a 'special audit report' (CA 1985, s247B) and modified notes to the accounts. The requirement for a special audit report will be waived where the company is exempt from appointing auditors.

ii Medium-sized companies

A medium-sized company is permitted to file an abbreviated profit and loss account and does not have to disclose details of profit and turnover in the notes to the accounts (CA 1985, s246A). A special audit report rather than a full audit report may be delivered.

iii Small and medium-sized groups

A parent company need not prepare group accounts where, for the financial year, the group qualifies as small or medium-sized and it is not an ineligible group (CA 1985, s248).

iv Dormant companies

With the exception of banking or insurance companies and authorised persons under the FSA 1986, which are outside the scope of these provisions, a company may qualify as 'dormant' where there have been no significant accounting transactions entered in the company's accounting records during the period concerned (CA 1985, new s249AA) and where the company:

- has been dormant since incorporation; or
- has been dormant since the end of the previous accounting year, qualifies as a small company (or would qualify if it was not a member of an ineligible group) and is not required to prepare group accounts.

A company that qualifies as dormant is able to claim all accounting exemptions applicable to small companies (see above) and can also automatically dispense with the requirement to appoint auditors without need for a special resolution. Companies House provides a very simple one-page format for dormant company accounts called 'DCA', which is available on request.

Public companies, previously excluded, may now qualify as dormant and claim dormant company exemptions when preparing their accounts (The Companies Act 1985 (Miscellaneous Accounting Amendments) Regulations 1996, SI 1996/189).

Audit exemptions

A private company that satisfies the criteria set out in CA 1985, ss249A and B (amended by the Companies Act 1985 (Audit Exemption) (Amended) Regulations 2000 (SI 2000/1430)) may be entitled to claim exemption from the requirement to have its annual accounts audited.

However, public companies, banks and insurance companies, authorised persons and appointed representatives under the FSA 1986, and special registered bodies or employers' associations registered under the Trade Union and Labour Relations (Consolidation) Act 1992 are ineligible for exemption from audit.

Before the exemption is applied, the directors must ensure that provisions in the company's Articles permit it to take advantage of the audit exemption. For example, Table A in Sch 1 to CA 1948 requires the appointment of auditors, and many companies have adopted detailed provisions for transfers of shares in their Articles that require independent valuation of the share price by the auditors. Where either of these provisions apply, the directors must ensure that a special resolution to amend provisions in the Articles is approved by the members before the company dispenses with the requirement to appoint auditors.

It is also important to note that, even where the company is not required to appoint auditors, the directors must ensure:

- proper accounting systems are maintained and adequate records are kept;
- the accounts prepared show a true and fair view and comply with provisions of the relevant Schedule to CA 1985 in terms of form and content;
- a directors' report is prepared as required by CA 1985;
- the annual report and accounts are submitted to Companies House within the correct period (see pages 74 and 75).

i Qualifying criteria

For a company to qualify for exemption from audit it must:

- qualify as a 'small' company in accordance with provisions of CA 1985, s247 (see page 75);
- have an annual turnover not exceeding £1 million net (CA 1985, s249A(2)). (The requirement for a report from a 'reporting accountant' has been repealed except where the small company is a charitable company with gross income of between £90,000 and £250,000);
- have a balance sheet total of not more than £1.4 million net.

If the company is a parent company or subsidiary, it will be exempt if the group qualifies as a small group (CA 1985, s249), is not ineligible and the group's aggregate turnover and aggregate balance sheet totals do not exceed the stated limits.

In addition, Regulation 2(7) of the Companies Act 1985 (Audit Exemption) (Amendment) Regulations 1997, SI 1997/936 clarifies that companies which are dormant and fall within CA 1985, s250 may claim exemption from audit either under that section or under CA 1985, s249A. Such companies are automatically entitled to exemption on the same terms as non-dormant qualifying companies.

ii Form of accounts

The form of the accounts must comply with provisions relating to small companies (except that no audit report is required) and will comprise an abbreviated balance sheet and modified notes to the accounts.

Requirements for the form and content of the accounts are set out in CA 1985, Schs 8 and 8A.

Where a company takes advantage of the audit exemption, the directors are required to include statements on the balance sheet that:

- the company was entitled to claim exemption under CA 1985, s249A(1);
- no notice has been received from the holders of 10% or more of the issued share capital (of any class) requiring an audit to be conducted (CA 1985, s249B(2));
- the directors acknowledge their responsibilities to keep proper accounting records and prepare accounts that show a true and fair account of the state of affairs of the company (in accordance with requirements of CA 1985, ss221 and 226);
- advantage has been taken of exemptions conferred by CA 1985, Part VII relating to small companies and that the company, in the opinion of the directors, is entitled to those exemptions.

Additional requirements for listed companies

In addition to the requirements to prepare, lay and deliver accounts set out above, there are a number of other requirements that directors of listed companies must ensure are observed.

i Preliminary statement of results

A listed company is required to announce a preliminary statement about its annual report and accounts to the Regulatory Information Service within 120 days of the end of the accounting period to which the accounts relate (Listing Rule 12.40) The 'preliminary results' must comprise a balance sheet, profit and loss account and cashflow statement and:

- must have been agreed with the auditors;
- be in table format consistent with the layout of the annual accounts;
- contain precise details of any dividend or distribution on listed securities;
- give details of any qualification made by the auditors;
- include any additional information necessary for shareholders and others to assess the accounts.

Failure to notify preliminary results within the required time may lead to a number of sanctions, including suspension of the company's securities.

ii Annual accounts

Directors of listed public companies must ensure that the annual accounts are published as soon as possible after approval and, in any event, not more than six months after the end of the accounting period to which they relate (Listing Rule 12.42(e)). Two copies of the accounts must be sent to the UK Listing Authority within this period.

Listing Rule 12.43 requires that the annual accounts contain the following additional information:

- An explanation of any difference of 10% or more on previously forecast results.
- A statement of the amount of interest capitalised, if any, and details of any related tax relief.
- Details of any waiver by directors of their emoluments in the current or future accounting periods.
- Details of any waiver of dividends by shareholders relating to the current or future accounting periods.
- Details of any change in directors' interests (distinguishing between beneficial and non-beneficial interests) between the beginning and end of the period and of any right to subscribe for shares or debentures. This information must be updated to within one month of the date of the notice of the AGM.
- A statement of information concerning major interests in shares (CA 1985, ss198–208) or a statement that there are no such interests.
- Details of any shareholder approval given for purchase of the company's own shares and of any purchases made during the period.
- Details of allotments for cash, including the name of allottees and market price of shares at the time of issue.
- Details of any undertaking given by the parent company (if any) where a placing was made during the period.
- Particulars of any significant contracts in which a director is or was materially interested.
- Particulars of any significant contracts made with a controlling shareholder during the period.
- Details of any small related party transactions during the period.
- Details of long-term incentive schemes (if any).
- A statement made by the directors and reviewed by the auditors that the company is a going concern. This may be included as a separate 'Going Concern Statement' or form part of the directors' report.

In addition, Listing Rule 12.43A requires the annual accounts to contain a Corporate Governance Statement, reviewed by the auditors, reporting on the extent of compliance with the Combined Code 2003 and effectiveness of the company's internal controls.

iii Summary financial statements

Directors of public companies whose shares are listed on the London Stock Exchange are permitted to send (either by post or electronic means) a summary financial statement (SFS) rather than full accounts to shareholders, debenture holders and other persons entitled to receive copies of the accounts and notice of meetings, provided such persons have indicated that an SFS is sufficient, or where they have not rejected proposals that it should be sent (CA 1985, S251). Details of the form and content required of the SFS are contained in the Companies (Summary Financial Statement) Regulations 1995 (SI 1995/2092).

Directors should note that, even where those entitled have indicated their acceptance of an SFS, they may at any time request a copy of the full accounts and reports, which must be supplied free of charge. The directors must ensure that the SFS is approved and signed by a director on behalf of the board and that a copy is sent to those entitled to receive it within the period required for delivering accounts.

iv Interim report

As well as the annual report and accounts, directors of companies with listed securities must also prepare an interim report (also referred to as a 'half yearly statement') detailing the activities and profit or loss made by the company in the first six months of the financial year (Listing Rule 12.46). The interim report must be announced to the Regulatory Information Service within 90 days of the end of the half year period to which it relates (Listing Rule 12.48).

Listing Rule 12.52 requires that the interim report comprises, essentially, a profit and loss account, balance sheet and cashflow statement, together with sufficient explanation to help understanding of performance, provide comparison with previous years and identify future prospects.

Whilst there is no requirement for the interim report to be audited, it is recommended by the Auditing Practices Board.

10 Health and safety

All companies have a duty to ensure the health, safety and welfare of employees whilst at work, which emanates from common law, the Health and Safety at Work etc. Act 1974 (HSWA 1974), the Management of Health and Safety at Work Regulations 1999 and numerous other regulations relating to specific work activities. This responsibility extends to:

- contractors whilst on the company's premises or carrying out work for the company *(Andrews v Initial Cleaning Services [2000] ICR 166)*;
- third parties using the company's goods or services, who should not be exposed to risks caused by an employee's negligence or lack of skill, experience or training *(R v Nelson Group Services (Maintenance) Ltd [1999] IRLR 646, CA)*;
- visitors, the general public and emergency services (HSWA 1974, ss2 and 3).

This chapter explains what directors must do to ensure the company fulfils its responsibilities in terms of health and safety, and covers:

- General duty
- Managing health and safety
- Risk assessment
- Health and safety policy
- Costs and penalties for breaches.

General duty

All employers must provide employees with safe conditions and systems of work and with appropriate training and supervision to enable them to perform their work safely (HSWA 1974, s2).

Because directors direct and control the company, they must make sure procedures are in place to ensure:

- safe equipment, plant and systems of work are provided and suitably maintained;
- articles and hazardous substances are safely used, handled, stored, transported and disposed of;

- employees receive instructions on how to carry out their work safely, supported by additional information, training and supervision where necessary;
- a safe working environment is provided.

There are numerous other regulations that impose duties on directors and the companies for which they act, whose application largely depends on the company's activities and employees' work. These include Provision and Use of Work Equipment Regulations 1998, Health and Safety (First Aid) Regulations 1981, Lifting Operations and Lifting Equipment Regulations 1999 and Construction (Health, Safety and Welfare) Regulations 1996, amongst many others.

Managing health and safety

Many companies traditionally considered health and safety issues at the operational management level. However, given that the directors make the strategic decisions likely to have significant health and safety implications, this level of delegation is now considered to have serious limitations. Consequently, it is increasingly recognised that there needs to be a formal assessment of health and safety risks. This should be considered by the board before any changes are implemented, in the same way that issues concerning finance, resource allocation, technical requirements, business interruption and regulatory requirements, etc. are considered.

This approach will be far from alien to most boards, especially those that have adopted the Turnbull Report's recommendations (see Chapter 2) and have implemented a broad risk-based approach to internal control.

To assist directors understand their responsibilities, the Health and Safety Commission (HSC) has issued the guidance entitled *Directors' Responsibilities for Health and Safety* (available from www.hse.gov.uk). It focuses on five key action points, namely the need for the board to:

- accept formally and publicly its collective role in providing health and safety leadership in its organisation;
- ensure its members accept their individual roles in providing health and safety leadership within the organisation;
- ensure that all board decisions reflect health and safety intentions stated in the health and safety policy (see page 86);
- recognise its role in engaging the active participation of staff in improving health and safety;

- be kept informed of, and alerted to, relevant health and safety risk management issues by appointing a health and safety director.

Whilst many of these responsibilities are included in existing health and safety legislation, for example the need to consult employees on specific health and safety matters, the action points are a succinct and effective way to bring them to the attention of busy directors and to ensure health and safety issues receive appropriate consideration.

Implications of these action points on the company's health and safety policy and risk assessments will be touched upon later in this chapter. The practical implications of recommendations to note here include:

- **Appointing a health and safety director.** By delegating responsibility for health and safety to one member of the board, that person will ensure the board always considers the health and safety issues arising from its decisions, in the same way that the finance director mentions finance restrictions or the operations director raises concerns over business interruption.

- **Leadership and support from individual directors.** It is very important for people both inside and outside the company to see from individual board members' actions and decisions that they are actively promoting good health and safety practice and that this is the culture to be followed within the company.

- **Consulting and involving employees.** Active employee participation with health and safety matters should be encouraged. This will help generate greater commitment amongst employees to achieving objectives and adhering to policies and procedures, improve their understanding of issues that affect them, and utilise their often valuable experience and knowledge when determining what procedures, means of communication, reporting and training will work best in practice.

- **Reviewing health and safety performance.** To keep the board informed of relevant health and safety risk management issues implementing a system of control is recommended, comprising a regular review of performance to identify any problems, investigating and reporting the causes and ensuring that preventative measures for managing the risks remain effective.

- **Reporting.** The HSC considers it good practice to report on corporate risk and health and safety issues in annual company reports and has issued guidance on how to do so (*Health and Safety* *in Annual Reports: Guidance from the Health and Safety Commission* – available from www.hse.gov.uk). Whilst the guidance is aimed initially at the FTSE top 350 companies, it will be extended to all businesses with more than 250 employees by 2004. Other companies would be well advised to adopt the proposals, thereby making the board publicly accountable for their management of health and safety risks.

Risk assessment

Regulations 3 and 4 of the Management of Health and Safety at Work Regulations 1999 require all employers formally to assess risks to employees whilst at work and implement arrangements for protective or preventative measures to reduce risks identified by the assessment. In addition, where five or more people are employed, the findings of the risk assessments must be recorded in writing.

Risk assessment is carefully examining what in a workplace could cause harm to people, following which the board can decide whether sufficient precautions have been taken to minimise the risk of injury or illness. Essentially the risk assessment process involves the following.

STAGE	PURPOSE
1 Examine characteristics of the workplace and activities being carried out.	To identify hazards that could cause harm.
2 Identify who could be harmed by the hazards identified and how.	To establish the likelihood of an injury occurring and quantify the severity of the risk and how many people could be affected.
3 Evaluate the risks in light of existing precautions.	To determine whether more could be done to remove or reduce the risks that injury may occur.
4 Record the findings and inform employees of the outcome.	To demonstrate that a proper check was carried out, problems were identified and appropriate corrective action taken.
5 Review and revise the assessment.	To ensure that recommended precautions have been implemented and are working effectively and to ensure that risks are assessed when new processes or equipment are implemented.

The sort of matters that would be examined in a risk assessment include what is involved in the employee's work activity, who is carrying out the work, the physical characteristics of the work area and environment, fire evacuation procedures, first aid provisions and arrangements for maintenance and servicing of equipment and security measures.

There are numerous other regulations requiring employers to carry out specific risk assessments, for example:

- Fire Precautions (Workplace) Regulations 1997 – risks relating to fire and precautionary measures in place;
- Control of Substances Hazardous to Health Regulations 2002 (as amended by SI 2003/978) – risks from exposure to hazardous substances;
- Health and Safety (Display Screen Equipment) Regulations 1992 – risks arising from working at a VDU workstation;
- Personal Protective Equipment at Work Regulations 1992 – assessment of personal protective equipment provided to carry out work safely;
- Manual Handling Operations Regulations 1992 – risks arising where manual handling cannot be avoided;
- Noise at Work Regulations 1989 – risks from exposure to noise.

The company's activities will determine which regulations apply. Many of the regulations include recommendations for 'best practice' and minimum performance standards.

Directors must ensure that an assessment of risks is carried out, as described above, to make sure no harm is caused to employees or others affected by the company's activities. There have been a number of successful cases brought against companies for failing to carry out risk assessments, resulting in harm caused to employees. For example, *Alexander v Midland Bank plc [1999] IRLR 723*, CA where employees suffered work related upper limb disorders attributed to their work activity and working practices; *Day v T Pickles Farm Ltd [1999] IRLR 217*, EAT where the employee successfully brought a claim for sex discrimination where the employer failed to carry out a risk assessment for pregnant women; *Walker v Northumberland County Council [1995] 1 AU ER 737* where the employer failed to carry out an assessment of risks relating to stress and breaching its duty of care gave rise to an employee's second stress-related breakdown.

Directors should also ensure this assessment of risks is carried out when decisions are made about doing business with other companies or employing sub-contractors. Whilst the initial cost of engaging certain companies may be attractive, where they are known to have a poor health and safety record and little or no means of managing health and safety risks there is a strong likelihood that this would undermine the company's good health and safety practice, potentially put the company's own employees at risk and ultimately damage the company's reputation. These factors should all be borne in mind.

Health and safety policy

Directors must be aware that where their company employs five or more people it has a statutory obligation to prepare and periodically review a formal written statement of the company's health and safety policy (HSWA 1974, s2(3)). The directors can be personally liable for failing to prepare and implement such a policy.

The policy must be communicated to employees via notice boards, posters, training and briefing sessions and during induction training for new recruits, and contain the following information: ·

- a general statement of the company's policy on health and safety, outlining the company's overall philosophy on health and safety and the broad responsibilities of management and the workforce;
- organisation for health and safety matters, detailing how responsibility is allocated to individuals for particular aspects of health and safety;
- a statement of arrangements and procedures for implementing the policy.

Directors must be aware that it is not enough merely to prepare this statement. They must ensure that arrangements are made to communicate the policy to employees and that activities are monitored on an ongoing basis to ensure that the manner in which work is carried out complies with the policy.

To adopt the HSC's recommended action points in respect of the health and safety policy, the directors must ensure:

- they clearly and publicly explain the board's responsibilities and commitment to achieving health and safety objectives in the health and safety policy and demonstrate how they will be achieved through organisation and procedures put into effect;

- the policy is not left to sit on the shelf gathering dust, but is a living document referred to as decisions are being made. It must be periodically updated to reflect changes within the company such as technology, processes and staff;.
- employees are consulted when devising the health and safety policy.

A further point for directors to note is that it is becoming increasingly common for customers and suppliers to ask to review a company's health and safety policy before deciding to engage in business. Consequently a well drawn up policy can in itself give the company a competitive advantage sufficient to secure new business.

Costs and penalties for breaches

The HSC has calculated that accidents and injuries at work cost British employers a staggering £3.3 to £6.5 billion a year.

Many employers misguidedly believe that most incidents will be covered by insurance. Whilst employer's liability insurance will (subject to any excess) meet the cost of serious injury to an employee (see Chapter 6), it would not usually cover costs incurred through:

- time away from work and loss of the injured person's production;
- payment of sick pay;
- arranging temporary cover;
- repairing plant and equipment;
- investigating the incident;
- imposition of fines;
- legal costs;
- loss of contracts;
- loss of business reputation.

Such uninsured costs can be substantial. Furthermore, employers with a poor record for health and safety claims may find that insurance premiums are substantially increased or, in some instances, that insurance cover is actually refused.

As well as avoiding the hidden costs of health and safety failures, many companies with high standards for health and safety have benefited from lower insurance premiums, improved levels of productivity and efficiency, improved quality of work, fewer staff absences and lower staff turnover. This is particularly important where investors, suppliers and customers are taking an increasing interest in the company's health and safety performance.

i Penalties – existing position

A breach of duty and failure to provide for the health and safety of employees constitutes both a criminal offence in terms of common law requirements and negligence and an offence giving rise to civil liability for breach of statutory requirements of HSWA 1974 and subsequent regulations. At present the maximum penalty for a breach of HSWA 1974 is £20,000 in the magistrates court, but higher in the Crown Court.

Under HSWA 1974, enforcing authorities have power to investigate suspected health and safety offences, which includes the right to search premises, take measurements, test equipment and take photographs. If the investigation shows that a company has failed to comply with the requirements of health and safety legislation, the Health and Safety Executive inspector may issue an improvement notice or, where the breach may involve serious risk of personal injury, a prohibition notice. Failure to comply with the notice is an offence for which the offender is liable for imprisonment, a fine, or both (HSWA 1974, s33).

Should an accident or incident have already occurred without the directors being aware of the need for improvement, both the company and its directors may be liable for:

- failure by the company to meet its obligations under HSWA 1974 s 2(1) by omitting to take reasonable precautions for employees' health, safety and welfare at work. The fines imposed for such breaches will reflect the seriousness of harm caused and how far short of the appropriate standard the employer's performance was. It should be noted that a company can be liable for a breach of duty at a lower or local management level even where head office is not aware of the offending actions (R v Gateway Foodmarkets Ltd [1997] IRLR 189, CA);
- corporate manslaughter, where it can be proven that a controlling officer had knowledge of the risks being taken. This was established in R v Kite, Stoddart and OLL Ltd, Winchester Crown Court, (8 December 1994, unreported), which involved a small company owned and run by the managing director whose actions were found to be criminally negligent in the face of obvious risks. The company was fined £60,000 for the offence;
- personal prosecution under HSWA 1974, s37, by which directors, or any person involved in the management of the company, may be

prosecuted where they are believed to have commissioned the offence, or where it can be proven to be attributable to their negligence. In the OLL case, above, the director was found guilty of manslaughter and jailed for three years. In *R v Rollco Screw and Rivet Co Ltd [1999] IRLR 439*, CA penalties were imposed on the company and the responsible directors personally for failing to remove asbestos from a building safely and breaching HSWA 1974, ss2(1) and 3(1). Personal prosecutions against directors used to be rare, however in 2000/01 out of 1,500 prosecutions brought against directors and managers, 45 were successful.

ii Penalties – proposed changes

It has been difficult in cases involving larger companies to establish existence of a 'controlling interest', necessary if a case for corporate manslaughter is to be pursued. This was certainly a problem following the Zeebrugge ferry disaster, the King's Cross fire in 1987, the Clapham rail crash in 1988, the Piper Alpha oil platform disaster in 1988, the sinking of the Marchioness in 1989, the Southall rail crash in 1998 and the Ladbroke Grove rail crash in 1999. Whilst each of these incidents involved a large number of deaths and casualties, attributed largely to management faults and allowing dangerous working practices to continue, no conviction for manslaughter proved possible because the existence of a 'controlling interest' could not be established.

However, on 23 May 2000 the Government published the consultation paper *Reforming the Law on Manslaughter: the Government's Proposals*, implementing the bulk of proposals made by the Law Commission (contained in the Involuntary Manslaughter Law Commission Report No 237) to create a new offence of 'corporate killing'. The Government has proposed that the new offence would be brought where a company's conduct causes a death and the conduct falls below what could 'reasonably be expected' in the circumstances without the need to establish a 'controlling interest'. Other implications of proposals relating to 'corporate killing' include:

- that the offence carries penalties comprising unlimited fines for both the corporation and any guilty officer;
- where the company is convicted of corporate killing, this should lead to disqualification of an individual found to have contributed

to or to have been responsible for management failure far below what could have been reasonably expected. The proposal is that this would apply not only to directors, but also to those involved in management of all types of undertakings;

- the possibility of imprisoning directors who contributed to the management failures that resulted in deaths.

The consultation paper also contains the Government's proposals for additional offences including:

- 'killing by gross carelessness', where the standard of an individual's conduct falls below what could 'reasonably be expected' and he or she is aware that such conduct could cause death or injury;
- 'reckless killing', where death results from a person's conscious decision to run the risk of causing death or injury;
- 'individual involuntary homicide', where death results from intentional or reckless causing of minor injury, i.e. where the resulting death was not foreseen.

These proposals have yet to be implemented. In the meantime, the Trade Union Congress and the Centre for Corporate Accountability have made further recommendations for directors to have legally binding health and safety responsibilities, including appointing a health and safety director, for directors to be liable for 'aiding and abetting' offences and for courts to have power to imprison convicted directors.

11 Stakeholders

As well as duties dictated by common law, those contained in the CA 1985 and related company legislation covered earlier, directors also have an extensive range of duties imposed by other statutes concerned with protecting the wider interests of company 'stakeholders'.

As well as shareholders, the term 'stakeholder' also covers employees, customers, creditors and the environment, all of which are affected by and have an interest in the company's activities and how its business is conducted.

Whilst directors' responsibilities towards stakeholders have for many years been embedded in statute, general awareness about them has perhaps not been as good as it should have been, largely due to the number and extensive range of statutes and regulations involved. For example, many directors would be surprised about the extent of their statutory liability for offences relating to environmental, employment or ethical matters.

More recently, directors' awareness of wider stakeholder interests and the need to communicate the company's performance in these areas has improved. This is partly as a result of initiatives such as:

- introduction of the Turnbull Report's recommendations for a risk-based approach to internal control, extending beyond mere financial controls to encompass areas such as environmental, health and safety and social risks;
- appointment by the Government of a Minister for Corporate and Social Responsibility;
- recommendations of the Company Law Review, now contained in the Companies Bill currently under consideration, for a statutory statement of directors' duties encompassing stakeholder issues;
- the requirement for occupational pension fund trustees to issue a statement of their investment policy, which involves obtaining information from the companies in which they invest about their performance with regard to social, environmental and ethical matters;

- developments in financial reporting standards, such as FRS 12, which requires the financial impact of certain environmental liabilities to be disclosed in the accounts;
- launch of the 'FTSE4Good' index to measure listed companies' performance in respect of social responsibility.
- the Tyson Report which, amongst other things, recommended that non-executive directors be recruited from more diverse backgrounds to widen the board's perspective, knowledge and understanding of stakeholder issues.

As well as statutory provisions that may impose a direct personal liability on directors to observe their duties to stakeholders, directors should also be aware that ignoring the interests of stakeholders may have a more indirect effect on the company's performance. This could include high staff turnover and poor productivity, reduced sales turnover as a result of bad publicity about products, or poor environmental performance, discouraging investors. This would undoubtedly have an effect on directors' remuneration and possibly their length of service with the company.

This chapter addresses directors' duties to stakeholders by covering basic duties towards:

- Employees
- The environment
- Customers
- Creditors.

In many cases the company's size will mean that directors delegate day-to-day responsibility for these matters to senior managers with specialist knowledge and experience. However, the directors must consider the implications for stakeholders of their policy and strategy decisions. They must also ensure that appropriate policies, procedures and controls are put in place to guide and monitor performance, and that those people dealing with these matters on a daily basis have the requisite knowledge, experience, training and information.

Employees

Essentially, employees sell their labour to companies in exchange for a salary and other benefits included in a contract. However, employees' rights contained in employment protection legislation now go well beyond the limits of this contractual relationship.

The directors are responsible for ensuring the company complies with the requirements of employment legislation. If they fail to do so, the aggrieved employee can make a claim against the company, not the directors. However, where the directors have acted fraudulently or have been negligent, the company may in turn make a claim against them for failure to act in the best interest of the company and to attend diligently to the company's affairs. Such counterclaim may be for a contribution to or an indemnity against the financial penalty incurred by the company.

Provisions in CA 1985, s309 place a general duty on directors to take regard of employees' interests in their management of the company. In practice it would be difficult not to observe this if the company is to attract and secure a workforce. The CA 1985 also requires that, where a company on average employs more than 250 employees in each week of the financial year, the directors must disclose the following information in the directors' report to the annual accounts:

- the company's policy on employment, training and advancement of disabled persons (CA 1985, Sch 7 Part III);
- arrangements made by the company during the year for involving employees in the company's affairs, policy and performance and for informing and consulting them on matters concerning employment (CA 1985, Sch 7 Part V).

If the necessary disclosures are not made, the directors in office immediately before the end of the relevant accounting period will be guilty of an offence and be liable to a fine (CA 1985, s234(5)).

As well as this general duty, the directors must also ensure they act in the best interests of the company in their treatment of employees, having regard to the following.

i The contract of employment

All employees working eight or more hours per week must receive a written statement of basic terms and conditions of employment (see Appendix 9) within two months of the start of their employment (ERA 1996, s1). A company with 20 or more employees must include details of the company's disciplinary and grievance procedures in the statement.

Additional provisions in the employment contract need to be carefully worded as they often increase the employee's benefits and at the same time increase the employee's obligations to the company. They may, for example, include requirements in relation to confidentiality of information, restrictive covenants, 'garden leave', extra benefits and ownership of intellectual property.

Once the terms of the contract have been agreed, the directors must ensure they are observed; if not the employee could make a claim for breach of contract.

ii Discrimination

Discrimination, victimisation and harassment, whether direct or indirect, against any person on the grounds of sex, race, disability or spent convictions is unlawful where it occurs at any time during the employment relationship. Given the potential for an Employment Tribunal to impose financial penalties on companies (including vicarious liability for other employees' discriminatory acts) as well as the potential for bad publicity, companies will be keen to avoid such proceedings.

A company must not be seen to endorse discriminatory acts. It is therefore important for directors to ensure that policies and procedures to address and discourage discrimination are implemented and communicated to employees. Such policies may include a code of practice to eliminate racial discrimination (recommended by the Commission for Racial Equality – see www.cre.gov.uk), an equal opportunities policy (recommended by the Equal Opportunities Commission – see www.eoc.org.uk), a discrimination and harassment policy and an appeals and grievance procedure.

iii Dismissal

Where there is a valid reason, directors may dismiss an employee from working for the company. For example in *Denco Ltd v Joinson [1991] IRLR 63 EAT*, dismissal of an employee for unauthorised use of a restricted computer file was considered gross misconduct and was deemed to have been fair. Similarly, an employer may dismiss an employee for reasons relating to capability, qualifications, conduct and redundancy.

However, unless the dismissal is for gross misconduct (other examples include theft and violence) and the employee is summarily dismissed, the employee must be made aware of the problem and be given the opportunity to improve before being dismissed. It is important that in each case employees are treated consistently and, to achieve this, directors are recommended to implement a formal disciplinary procedure, identifying clear rules and steps to be taken that could lead up to dismissal. The ACAS *Code of Practice on Disciplinary and Grievance Procedures* provides guidance on how to draw up disciplinary rules and procedures and operate them effectively. It can be downloaded from www.acas.org.uk

Employees also have statutory rights to protect them from 'unfair' dismissal (ERA 1996, s94). For example, dismissal will be considered automatically unfair where it:

- is connected with maternity;
- followed the employee seeking to assert an employment right, such as the right to receive the minimum wage (National Minimum Wage Act 1998);
- arises when an employee attempts to take action on health and safety grounds;
- follows a transfer of undertaking;
- arises by the employee refusing to work on Sundays;
- occurs due to an employee's membership or non-membership of a trade union;
- follows proceedings brought against the employer by a part-time employee refusing to accept less favourable treatment than a full-time employee.

Where an employee's claim is successful and dismissal is judged to have been unfair, the employee may be awarded up to £50,000 as compensation for dismissal (ERA 1999, ss 33–37). This award may be even higher where the employer refuses to reinstate the employee, and where the dismissal followed a protected disclosure ('blowing the whistle') by the employee, under the Public Interest Disclosure Act 1998, may be limitless.

Directors must be aware of the overall constraints on dismissal of employees and ensure that a formal disciplinary policy is implemented and followed.

iv Data protection

The structured and personal nature of a company's employment records means that they come within the scope of the DPA 1998. The directors must ensure that notification about processing made to the Information

Commissioner includes employment records, and that the eight data protection principles (set out in Appendix 10) are observed at all times.

To assist employers understand the impact of data protection requirements on processing of an employee's personal data, the Information Commissioner issued the *Employment Practices Data Protection Code* setting out recommendations for how organisations can adhere to the requirements of the DPA 1998. The code (available from www.dataprotection.gov.uk) comprises four parts:

- Part 1 – recruitment and selection and employment practices;
- Part 2 – records management;
- Part 3 – monitoring at work; and
- Part 4 – medical information (not yet available).

Directors would be well advised to ensure the recommendations made by the Information Commissioner are observed, as they provide a benchmark against which alleged breaches of the DPA 1998 will be judged.

The practical measures directors should ensure are implemented include limiting access to employees' personal data, keeping records up-to-date, only collecting, processing and retaining information that is relevant to the employment relationship, and controlling to whom and how the information is released. Also, employees have a right to see information being held about them, within 40 days of their request.

Where an offence has been committed by the company with the consent or connivance of the directors, or it has occurred as a result of their neglect, the directors will be guilty of the offence alongside the company and be liable on summary conviction to a fine (DPA 1998, ss60 and 61). It is also a criminal offence to process personal data without notification, and a person may be entitled to claim compensation for damage caused as a result of breach of the DPA 1998.

v Restrictions on who can be employed

Directors should be aware that, in a few instances the company is restricted in whom it employs. For example:

- It is an offence to employ a person who is not entitled to work in the UK (Asylum and Immigration Act 1996, s8). A fine of up to £5,000 may be imposed on the company or its directors and officers where they connived in the offence or it arose as a result of their neglect. To prevent prosecution directors must ensure that, as part of the usual recruitment process, no person is allowed to commence work without providing evidence of their entitlement to work in the UK, such as a P45, passport confirming citizenship, birth certificate or Home Office letter confirming their right to work.

• Subject to certain exceptions and restrictions, employment of children aged under 13 years is prohibited, and employment of young people between school-leaving age and 18 years is subject to restrictions, for example in terms of hours and suitable work (Children and Young Persons Act 1933, as amended by SI 1998/276 and SI 2000/1333).

The environment

An expansive range of 'green' legislation has extended a company's responsibility to avoid pollution and protect the environment well beyond civil liability for environmental damage (established in common law by *Rylands v Fletcher [1861–73] All ER Rep 1*). It imposes criminal liability on the company for infringement, as well as making directors personally liable for offences committed with their consent or connivance, or resulting from their neglect.

Statutory provisions are now largely consolidated in the Environmental Protection Act 1990, the Environment Act 1995 and, more recently, the Pollution Prevention and Control (England and Wales) Regulations 2000 (SI 2000/1973). They set down requirements for 'preventing' pollution, which encompass emissions into the air, water quality and effluent waste, solid waste (including toxic and radioactive substances), smoke, dust, steam, gas, and fume emissions, noise pollution, litter, and disposal of waste, etc. Directors should also be aware that other legislation, such as the COSHH Regulations 1999 governing the supply, use, storage and disposal of hazardous substances, and COMAH Regulations 1999 on the prevention and limitation of the effects of major accidents, are intrinsically linked to environmental protection.

Directors need to consider the company's operations and the effects of its activities on the environment. This assessment would usually form part of the company's overall risk management process, as not only could damage to the environment expose the company to heavy financial penalties, including costs for cleaning up contaminated land (EPA 1990, Part IIA), but it may also attract bad publicity and damage the company's reputation, result in a ban on the company's activities and discourage potential investors and customers.

Whilst directors of, say, an industrial or manufacturing company will undoubtedly be aware of the importance of environmental protection and implications for their companies, it may not be so apparent for the directors of a lower risk, office-based non-manufacturing company. However, even in the last instance there are environmental protection matters that need consideration, for example:

- disposal of paper waste as, if there are no arrangements for recycling or recovery, the company has to make suitable waste disposal arrangements and pay Landfill Tax;
- how much and what type of packaging is used, as many companies have an obligation to reduce the amount of packaging waste sent to landfill sites (Producer Responsibility Obligations (Packaging Waste) Regulations 1997) and to minimise the use of noxious or hazardous substances in packing and improve recycling, re-use or recoverability of packaging (the Packaging (Essential Requirements) Regulations 1998 (SI 1998/1165)).

Given that, in varying degrees, all companies must consider the need for protection of the environment, key practical issues for directors include the following.

i Planning

EA 1995, s5 requires companies to assess levels of pollution arising from their activities and to pre-determine measures that will be implemented where it becomes apparent they need to prevent, minimise, remedy or mitigate pollution. Again this forms an important part of a company's risk management process.

ii Authorisation

There are certain processes with an inherent risk of harm to the environment that require authorisation, and the company must obtain a licence before such activities commence (EPA 1990, s2(1)). Where such authorisation is obtained, the company's activities will be regulated and emissions will need to be monitored. Should the company then breach the conditions of authorisation, an enforcement or prohibition notice may be issued (EPA 1990, ss13 and 14).

It is an offence to fail to obtain authorisation, where required, or to exceed maximum omission limits, and in such cases action may be taken against the directors as well as or instead of the company (EPA 1990, ss157(1) and 158 and other relevant environmental legislation). For example, the managing director of Pharmacos was disqualified from acting as a director for four years (CDDA, 1986) and was personally fined £2,500 and ordered to pay costs of £3,500 for unlawfully operating a prescribed process under EPA 1990, Part I (*Environmental Data Services Report 299, December 1999*).

iii Setting standards and monitoring performance

The Environment Agency has statutory powers to regulate and control pollution, inspect premises and impose bans where it finds operating methods need to be changed or where further controls are necessary to prevent or minimise the risk of pollution.

It is therefore important for the directors to ensure that standards for environmental performance are set, appropriate measures to achieve them are implemented and actual performance is measured against the targets to identify potential problems at the earliest opportunity. Many companies aim to achieve this by implementing:

- **environmental policies** – these vary enormously, from a single-page statement of intent to basic guidelines and voluminous policy manuals. Often there are separate stand-alone policies, each setting targets and objectives for specific aspects of environmental performance such as disposal of waste, energy conservation and air and water pollution;
- **environmental management systems** – this is a more integrated approach to environmental management, based on the environmental policy but extending further to address organisation of personnel and management, details of statutory requirements, clear objectives and targets, operational controls, record systems, audits and reviews.

Whilst neither of these is a statutory requirement, customers and suppliers often ask to see evidence of a company's environmental policy, production of which may be a condition of business. Other possible benefits include creating a competitive advantage by improving perception of the company's 'integrity' amongst investors, customers, employees, analysts, etc., lower insurance premiums and improved relations with environmental regulators who can see that the company is committed to minimising damage to the environment.

iv Reporting

Whilst there is no statutory requirement at present, directors and those involved in the management of companies are under increasing pressure to account and demonstrate to shareholders, investors, pressure groups, customers and employees, etc. that the company is taking steps to protect the environment. For example, a number of shareholder pressure groups and pension fund managers have indicated that they will vote against receipt of the annual accounts of any FTSE 100 company that does not contain an environmental report.

In addition, government ministers have expressed dissatisfaction at the number of companies with more than 250 employees that lag behind implementing and reporting on progress under environmental policies and have warned that if this does not improve a mandatory standard may be imposed.

Customers

Directors will be aware that they have extensive duties to a company's customers which must be observed, not only to reduce the potential for litigation but also to preserve the company's corporate image and obtain new and repeat sales. Duties to customers include the following.

i Product safety

It is a fundamental requirement that all products placed on the market must be safe. Therefore extensive product research and testing needs to be carried out before products are placed on sale.

The ramifications and costs of contravening this requirement can be substantial. Not only will the goods need to be withdrawn from sale and those already sold be recalled, but also a penalty of up to £5,000, three months' imprisonment, or both may be imposed (General Product Safety Regulations 1994). The company as the producer, supplier or importer of the goods will have strict criminal liability for damage caused by the defect.

Directors should also be aware that prohibition and suspension notices can be issued to prevent supply and sale of defective goods (CPA

1987, ss13 and 14) and action can be taken where goods are sub-standard or of a lower quality that expected (Sale of Goods Act 1979 and Sale and Supply of Goods Act 1994 amongst others).

In addition, the Sale and Supply of Goods to Consumers Regulations 2002 (SI 2002/3045) provide consumers who have purchased faulty goods, with the right to rely on a statement made by any business in the supply chain, a guarantee whether or not it was intended to be legally binding, and to request that the goods be repaired or replaced or that a full refund be given.

ii Accurate trade descriptions

All advertising – on packaging, in sales literature and in statements made by sales staff – must describe goods accurately in terms of their physical characteristics, price, quantities, weights and sizes, fitness for purpose, etc. (TDA 1968 and CPA 1987, Part III).

The company has criminal liability where a false description of goods has been given. The directors may also be held personally liable where the offence was committed with their knowledge or consent, or was due to their negligence, and may face a fine of up to £2,000, two years' imprisonment, or both (TDA 1968, s20 and CPA 1987, s2).

iii Fair contract terms

The Unfair Terms in Consumer Contracts Regulations 1994 (SI 1994/3159) require contracts to be fair, and invalidate any unfair terms in contracts that have not been individually negotiated, such as a clause allowing the supplier not to fulfil his or her obligations fully. Directors should therefore ensure that wording of the company's standard contracts is clear and easy to understand, and does not contain clauses that would be considered unfair.

Regulation 15 of the Sale and Supply of Goods Regulations 2002 also states that where goods are sold or otherwise supplied to a consumer with a guarantee, the guarantee shall take effect as a contractual obligation.

Having read what is required, directors would therefore be well advised to carry out a full legal audit of all existing agreements with customers, suppliers and competitors to ensure they comply. They must also ensure that those responsible for negotiating contract terms are aware of and observe these requirements.

iv Consumer protection

Provisions protecting consumers against unfair trading practices and anti-competitive behaviour are mainly embodied in the Enterprise Act 2002 (which largely replaced the Fair Trading Act 1973) and the Competition Act 1998. Particular practices which directors must ensure are avoided include:

- **anti-competitive agreements** – prohibited by the Competition Act 1998, which permits the Office of Fair Trading ('OFT') to impose a financial penalty of up to 10% of an offending company's turnover for three years. In addition, competitors and customers may seek compensation for damages and, where directors obstruct investigations, they themselves may face unlimited fines or up to two years' imprisonment;
- **abuse of a dominant market position** – the Competition Act 1998 prohibits monopolists limiting production, markets or technical development to the detriment of the consumer. For example, Napp Pharmaceuticals Limited of Cambridge was fined £3.21 million for abusing its dominant market position in its pricing practices.
- **criminalisation of cartels** – in addition to the imposition on the company of civil sanctions permitted by the Competition Act 1998 for the operation of cartels and anti-competitive agreements, the Enterprise Act 2002 now makes it a criminal offence for an individual to dishonestly engage in cartel agreements. Directors face personal liability where they or their undertakings engage in price-fixing, limitations of supply or production, market sharing or bid-rigging.
- **offering bribes to secure business** – this has long been an offence in the UK and the Anti-Terrorism and Security Act 2001 now makes it an offence to pay a bribe overseas, including gratuities and small 'facilitating payments'.

Directors should note that the OFT and trading standards authorities have power to enforce consumer legislation and to require a trader to stop a course of conduct which is unlawful and detrimental to consumers. The OFT must first consult with the offending business to get them to stop the infringing conduct. Where this is not successful, application can be made to the court for an Enforcement Order (EO). Should a person breach the requirements of an EO, he or she will be in contempt of court and liable to a fine and imprisonment. For example, EOs can be issued where a business is required to change its practice and has failed to do so in respect of advertising, use of unfair contract terms, or the way it sells and supplies its goods.

As mentioned in Chapter 13, the OFT has the power to seek disqualification of a director where serious breaches of competition law are established. Alternatively the OFT may accept a competition disqualification undertaking from a director.

Directors must ensure that policies, procedures, management systems and codes of conduct are implemented to discourage and prevent unfair trading practices. They could not only be facing personal liability and penalties for anti-competitive behaviour, but also a successful conviction could seriously damage a company's reputation for integrity and fair trading and, either directly or indirectly, lead to a loss of customers and quality staff and make it difficult to raise capital from the investment community.

v Marketing and advertising

Directors must be aware that provisions in the Telecommunications (Data Protection and Privacy) (Direct Marketing) Regulations 1998 and the Telecommunications (Data Protection and Privacy) Regulations 1999 make it an offence to send unsolicited direct marketing faxes or to make unsolicited telephone calls (by automated system) to an individual without their prior consent. This has had a profound effect on how companies promote themselves through direct marketing as individuals have a statutory right to opt out of receiving marketing faxes and calls, and companies can opt-out of receiving unsolicited faxes. Such opt-out requests must be observed.

The Consumer Protection (Distance Selling) Regulations 2000 place restrictions on the way companies sell goods by phone, the internet, mail order, email, etc. without any personal contact with the customer. These restrictions must be observed and, in brief, include requirements to provide clear information, confirm this information in writing, allow a seven-day 'cooling off' period in which the order can be cancelled and supply the goods within 30 days.

The Privacy and Electronic Communications (EC Directive) Regulations 2003 (SI 2003/2426) came into force on 11 December 2003 making it an offence to send an 'individual subscriber' unsolicited commercial e-mails or text messages.

There are also around 100 UK statutes, orders and regulations setting out requirements for advertising and promotions that must be observed, as a breach may give rise to criminal prosecution or civil action. Directors should ensure that those responsible for advertising are aware of the restrictions placed upon them and that appropriate controls are in place to ensure all advertisements and promotions are accurate, ethical, do not mislead, offend or contain unacceptable comparisons and meet all requirements of legislation and the Advertising Standards Authority's code of practice. Having to amend or withdraw advertisements is not only costly but can also attract damaging publicity.

vi Protection of personal data

Personal data about individual personal customers needs to be protected in the same way as data about employees and others who have dealings with the company, and principles of the DPA 1998 (set out in Appendix 10) must be observed.

For example, if an individual has provided personal details to receive a brochure about a company's products, that information should not be used for another purpose such as cross-selling by other companies in the group, unless the individual has given consent.

The need to observe data protection principles such as keeping the information up-to-date and secure make sound sense from a commercial point of view as not only will information be sent to the right address, but a company's client list is a valuable asset that needs protection against access by third parties and competitors. Consequently, as well as the need to avoid an offence being committed under the DPA 1998, good management of data can have very positive benefits for the company.

vii Selling goods on credit

Most businesses that offer goods or services on credit or lend money to consumers must obtain a credit licence (Consumer Credit Act 1974). Not only is it a criminal offence to make such transactions without a licence, which is punishable by fine, imprisonment or both, but the company may also be left exposed as the unlicensed agreement may be unenforceable.

Creditors

A company must be able to pay for the goods and services it acquires and meet its debts as they fall due. If at any time this is not the case, or there is a change in the conditions under which the creditor agreed to do business with the company, the directors must inform the creditors. To protect the interests of creditors, directors therefore have a duty to:

- enter into contracts for goods or services only when there is a reasonable prospect that the company will be able to pay for them;
- inform creditors of any payment out of capital for purchase by the company of its own shares as, in the event of a winding-up, this will reduce the company's ability to repay amounts owing to creditors.

Two important developments for creditors in recent years include the requirement for a company to include a statement about the company's practice, policy and performance on payment of creditors in the directors' report to the annual accounts (CA 1985, Sch 7 Part VI) (unless exempt – see Chapter 9) and the Late Payment of Commercial Debts (Interest) Act 1998 allowing qualifying companies to charge interest on overdue payments.

Both developments have important implications for directors. In the first instance, information on payment performance disclosed in the accounts may influence a supplier's decision on whether to do business with the company and, in the second, a company may need to review its payment policy to keep the cost of supplies to a minimum by avoiding interest on late payments.

12 The struggling company

Provisions have been introduced into the IA 1986 to deter improper activities by directors when a company is struggling as a going concern and faces the possibility of liquidation. Damage to creditors can be extensive and duties contained in the IA 1986 are devised to encourage directors to take early action to minimise the loss to creditors. To focus the directors' attention, the IA 1986 also introduced personal liability by requiring directors to contribute to the assets of a company on winding-up where they have committed certain statutory offences (see Chapter 13). On 15 September 2003, the Enterprise Act 2002 introduced new Schedule B1 to replace existing provisions in Part II of the IA 1986 on administration and its entirety.

This chapter covers directors' duties in relation to:

- Voluntary arrangement
- Administration
- Liquidation.

Voluntary arrangement

If a company is experiencing difficult trading conditions and the directors reasonably believe that, with 'breathing space', changes could be implemented to allow the company to continue trading. The company could enter into a voluntary arrangement with its creditors (IA 1986, s1). This may, for example, include reaching agreement with creditors on the proportion of debts they will be paid, followed by a scheme of arrangement for the company's affairs by, say, selling off part of the business to allow it to continue trading. Once a voluntary arrangement has been agreed the company's trading can continue and each party to the agreement must abide by the terms.

The proposal would usually be put by the directors to the company's shareholders and its creditors for approval based upon representations and proposals from the directors (IA 1986 ss1 and 3). If any director or officer makes false representations to obtain approval of the voluntary arrangement, he or she will be liable to imprisonment, a fine, or both (IA 1986, s6A(4)).

Administration

Part 10 of the Enterprise Act 2002 came into force on 15 September 2003 changing IA 1986 by substituting a new Part II on administration and introducing new Schedule B1. These changes have been made to facilitate the rescue of struggling companies wherever possible and to restrict the use of administrative receivership and encourage the use of administration which collectively takes account of the interests of all creditors rather than just one.

Entry into administration is now possible by appointment of an administrator by the:

- court, on application by the company, its directors, one or more creditor, or a magistrate's court (IA 1986, Sch B1, paras 11–13). This may well remain the preferred route into administration for larger and more complex cases;
- holder of a floating charge (IA 1986, Sch B1, para 14); or
- company or its directors (IA 1986, Sch B1, para 22)

In each case there are procedures that must be followed and information that must be provided for the administration to take effect. The last two means of entry described above do not require a court application or hearing, making them a quicker and less costly alternative.

Once the administrator has been appointed, the administration process is the same for all classes and the administrator has the duty to act in the interests of all creditors.

Directors should note that the Enterprise Act 2002 introduced the requirement that, unless an extension has been arranged, administration will cease automatically at the end of one year from the date it took effect (IA 1986, Sch B1, para 76).

In each of the above instances the directors will be required to provide a true and accurate statement of the company's affairs to the administrator, containing details of assets, debts and liabilities, creditors' names and addresses, securities held by creditors and any other information relevant to administration (IA 1986, Sch B1, para 47(1)). Failure to provide information requested, or to conceal any information or make a false statement is an offence giving rise to imposition of a fine (IA 1986, Sch B1, para 48(4)).

Furthermore, the directors must ensure that every invoice, order for goods, business letter and other document on which the company's name appears clearly states that the company is in administration (IA 1986, Sch B1, para 45(1)). Failure to show this information is an offence for which the directors, as well as the administrator, will be liable to pay a fine.

Liquidation

Where a company, for whatever reason, is not able or permitted to continue in operation, application may be made to the court for the company to be placed in liquidation and be wound up.

The company may be wound up voluntarily by the members, where the directors can declare that the company is solvent and will remain so for at least 12 months, or by the court or the creditors where it is not solvent.

As well as needing to follow set procedures leading up to the appointment of a liquidator, once the liquidator has been appointed directors have certain duties to co-operate with them and supply information (as detailed in Appendix 11). The directors must fulfil these duties to avoid claims that they have acted against the interests of creditors. In addition, case law has established that directors must co-operate proactively rather than reactively with liquidators by, for example, supplying information they know to be relevant rather than waiting to be asked to supply it (*R v McCredie [2000] 2 BCLC 438*).

Importantly, once the company is placed in liquidation the actions of the directors will be subject to close scrutiny, especially where the company is insolvent and unable to pay its debts. Matters that will receive particular attention include whether there is evidence that the directors:

- gave preferential treatment to particular creditors when settling their debts (IA 1986, s239);
- entered into any transactions at an undervalue and did not receive adequate consideration for the company at a time when it was unable to pay its debts (IA 1986, 238);
- misappropriated any of the company's money or property or were guilty of any misfeasance or breach of duty (IA 1986, s212);
- conducted the business of the company with a dishonest intent to defraud creditors or for any other fraudulent purpose (fraudulent trading);

- allowed the company to continue to trade where they knew, or ought to have known, that the company had no reasonable prospect of avoiding insolvent liquidation (wrongful trading) and did not take every step necessary to minimise the potential loss to creditors (IA 1986, s21).

Where directors are found to have committed any of these offences, depending on the offence, they may be personally liable to contribute to the company's assets, be fined, imprisoned or both, or be disqualified from acting as a director (see Chapter 13).

Whilst these penalties alone are quite severe, there are proposals in the Enterprise Act 2002 to increase penalties on reckless and culpable bankrupts who fail to give consideration to a company's creditors by imposing 'bankruptcy restriction orders' to last for up to 15 years, and possible imprisonment.

13 Penalties for breach of duty

Directors who have breached either common law or statutory duties may face:
- Dismissal
- Action for breach of common law duties
- Action for breach of statutory duties
- The need to ratify the breach of duty.

Each is discussed in this chapter, and emphasise the importance of directors fulfilling their duties and highlight instances when they are not protected from the company's limited liability.

Dismissal

If members of the company become aware and are concerned that a director is not carrying out his or her duties in relation to the company and its affairs, is not acting in the best interests of the company, or is in some way bringing the company into disrepute, they may consider it necessary to remove the director from office to protect the company – either financially or otherwise. Whatever the circumstances, the members have power to remove a director by ordinary resolution, as set out in Chapter 3.

Action for breach of common law duties

Directors who breach their fiduciary duty or duty of skill and care to the company will be liable to civil action instigated by the party to whom the duty is owed (most often the company) for any loss suffered or undisclosed profit made or advantage taken. The company may consider it appropriate that the director's breach of duty be ratified after the event, permissible in certain circumstances (see page 120), or may take legal action to obtain:
- an injunction to restrain the director and prevent him or her from carrying out or continuing with the action constituting the breach of duty;

- damages by way of compensation where the director's action is considered negligent;
- restoration of the company's property, provided it does not prejudice an innocent third party, where the director's fiduciary duty has been broken and assets have been misappropriated;
- an account of profits made by the director;
- rescindment of a contract in which the director has an undisclosed interest;
- the director's dismissal.

For example:

- in *Guinness plc v Saunders [1988] 2 All ER 940* the director failed to observe his fiduciary duty to the company by entering a contract for his own personal benefit and by making a secret profit, and the company successfully pursued action for repayment of the director's profit to the company;
- in *CMS Dolphin Ltd v Simonet [2001] 2 BCLC 704* a director who persuaded former clients to transfer their business to a new company after his resignation was in breach of his fiduciary duty and personally liable for resulting profits.

Most importantly, directors who commit wrongful acts in the course of their duties cannot shelter under the protection of a company and, if found guilty of fraud, misrepresentation or other tort, will be personally liable alongside the company. A director's duty to exercise skill and care is commonly called into question in respect of statements and information issued on behalf of the company to third parties, for example in brochures, accounts, circulars, prospectuses and offer documents. Where such statements are found to contain inaccurate, misleading, false or unsubstantiated information the directors may be liable for breach of duty and face:

- a civil claim for negligence if the misstatements are made as a result of careless omission or neglect;
- criminal penalties where there is evidence of intentional fraud or recklessness.

Where a director is found to have abused his or her position as 'trustee' of the company's assets and has misapplied them in any way, provisions of IA 1986, s212 permit the liquidator to pursue the director for restoration of the company's property and for payment of the money involved or compensation. Furthermore, where, in the course of winding up it transpires that the company's business has been conducted with intent to defraud creditors, itself considered as misapplication of funds, the court may impose personal liability on those directors party to the fraud for all debts and liabilities of the company, without limitation.

However, under the CA 1985, s727, if the court considers that a director acted honestly and reasonably, having regard to all the circumstances, it has the power to exempt a director from action for negligence, default, breach of duty or breach of trust.

Action for breach of statutory duties

Many statutes impose duties on directors. Each includes provisions detailing criminal or civil sanctions for breach of such duties. The CA 1985, Sch 24 alone lists some 250 offences. Other statutes with sanction for offences committed by directors include the Theft Act 1968 (obtaining property or pecuniary advantage by deception), the Criminal Justice Act (CJA) (dealing in company securities at a time when they have 'insider knowledge'), IA 1986 (fraudulent and wrongful trading) and the Trades Descriptions Act (TDA) 1968 (making misleading trade descriptions to consumers).

Unless specifically stated in the relevant statute, criminal liability for acts of the company rests with the company and not the directors. However, directors should be aware that:

- many sub-sections of CA 1985 make '*every officer of the company who is in default*' accountable for the offence (including 'shadow' and 'de facto' directors) and most often the directors will be first in line because of their position in the company. The nature of accountability will be specified in the relevant section and may be a fine, imprisonment or both;
- some requirements of CA 1985 are the directors' responsibility, for example delivering annual accounts to Companies House (s242), disclosing their interests in shares (s324) and disclosing interests in contracts to be made with the company (s317). As a result the directors are personally responsible for ensuring compliance.

Directors should be aware that the courts are now enforcing severe penalties on directors who fail to meet their statutory obligations and, should their conduct be called in to question, they may face personal liability or disqualification.

i Personal liability

As illustrated in the table below, there is an extensive range of circumstances where directors may find themselves personally liable to third parties for loss resulting from their acts or omissions in managing the company and for statutory offences committed by them.

OFFENCE COMMITTED	STATUTORY PROVISION/ CASE EXAMPLE
Making false or misleading statements or omitting information from listing particulars or a prospectus	FSMA 2000, s90(1) for loss resulting from listing particulars supporting an application for the admission of securities to the UK Listing Authority's Official List and under s14 of the Public Offer of Securities Regulations 1995 (SI 1995 1537) from a prospectus relating to unlisted securities
Irregularities in allotments	CA 1985, s85(2)
Fraudulent trading	CA 1985, s458
Failing to show the company name clearly on bills of exchange, promissory notes, endorsements, cheques or orders for money (the director is liable to the third party where the company fails to pay)	CA 1985, s349 (*Barber and Nicholls Ltd v R&G Associates (London) Ltd and Rogers [1981] CA Transcript 455, 132 NLJ 1076*, where the company name was incorrectly stated on a cheque and on default by the company, the director who signed the cheque was held personally liable)
Failure to observe shareholders' rights of pre-emption	CA 1985, s92
Failure to obtain a trading certificate for a public company before entering into a transaction with a third party	CA 1985, s117
Where, in winding up the business of the company, it becomes apparent that it has been conducted with intent to defraud	CA 1986, s213

Where guilty of 'wrongful trading'	IA 1986, s214 (*Official Receiver v Doshi (2001) 2 BCLC 235* where a director responsible for wrongful trading was ordered to make an appropriate contribution to the company's assets)
Where a director of an insolvent company carries on business using a prohibited name	IA 1986 ss216 and 217 *(Archer Structures Ltd v Griffiths [2003] All ER (D) 172 (May), ChD)*
Non-payment of betting or gaming duties by the company	Betting and Gaming Duties Act 1981 *(Customs and Excise Comrs v Hedon Alpha Ltd [1981] QB 818 [1981] 2 All ER 697 CA)*
Fraudulent evasion of VAT	FA 1986, s14 *(Customs and Excise Comrs v Bassimeh [1995] STC 910)*
Making a dishonest declaration or failing to register for VAT	FA 1986, s13(1) *(Stevenson and Telford Building and Design Ltd v Customs and Excise Comrs [1996] STC 1096, CA)*
Employing illegal immigrants and overstayers	Asylum and Immigration Act 1996 (fine of up to £5,000)
Deliberately driving the company into liquidation to avoid NI debts	Criminal Justice Act 1988 (Confiscation Orders) Order 1996 (SI 1996/1716)
Failure to pay NI	Criminal Justice Act 1988 (SI 1996/1716) under which an order can be made freezing assets of officers of a company which intentionally failed to pay NI
Knowingly giving preference to a creditor on a winding up	IA 1986 ss238-240 *(Re Living Images Ltd [1996] 1 BCLC 348, [1996] BCC 112)*
Acting as a director whilst disqualified	CDDA 1986 s 15
Health and safety offences	Health and Safety at Work, etc. Act 1974 *(R v Rollco Screw and Rivet Co Ltd [1999] 2 Cr App Rep (S) 436, CA* where directors were fined for asbestos contamination)

| Authorising payment of an illegal dividend | *Bairstow v Queens Moat Houses Plc,* *[2000] 1 BCLC 549* |
| For paying a loan to a director without disclosure and approval of the shareholders | CA 1985, s330 *(Currencies Direct Ltd v Ellis (2001) Times, 27 November, QBD)* in which it was held a loan to a director could be recovered) |

As well as the statutory offences listed above, directors who may have personal liability to third parties should be also aware of the following instances where they may be held personally liable:

- where they fail to make their capacity as an 'agent' for the company clear when contracting with a third party, they may find themselves liable where the company defaults or breaches the contract;
- where they have personally guaranteed the company's obligations under a contract or arrangement, such as a bank overdraft;
- for payment of fines to industry regulators, for example under FSMA 2000, the UK Listing Authority may fine directors personally for breaches of the Listing Rules;
- to account to the company for any loss or damage suffered by their failure to observe their duties to the company. For example, where the directors authorise a loan to a director contrary to provisions of CA 1985, s330, they are likely to face civil action for restitution of money as well as criminal liability for their actions. Similarly, they would be held liable to repay monies to the company for contracts in which they failed to disclose their interest (CA 1985, s320) and to compensate the company where, in the course of a winding-up, it is apparent that they have misappropriated any of the company's money or property (IA 1986 s 212).

ii Disqualification

Although provisions enabling courts to disqualify persons from acting as directors have been in force for many years, the number of disqualifications is on the increase – in the nine month period to 31 December 2001 1,298 directors were disqualified. From this statistic, it is clear that directors who fail to meet their duties face a very realistic threat of disqualification.

The law regarding disqualification of directors is consolidated in CDDA 1986 and allows for:

- automatic disqualification as an outcome of defined events or occurrences;
- application to be made to the court for a disqualification order.

Where a director has failed to meet obligations required by other legislation, such as CA 1985, FSMA 2000, IA 1986 or HSWA 1974, an application may be made for a disqualification order under the relevant section of CDDA 1986.

Implications of a disqualification order

Once disqualified, the person who is the subject of the disqualification order may not, without leave of the court, be a director of a company, act as receiver of a company's property or as an insolvency practitioner, or directly or indirectly be concerned with or take part in the promotion, formation or management of a company (CDDA 1986, s1). These same restrictions apply where a person has given a voluntary disqualification undertaking (CDDA 1986, s1A).

It is a criminal offence to act in contravention of a disqualification order, punishable by legal process with up to two years' imprisonment or an unlimited fine.

The name of anyone disqualified will appear on the 'register of disqualified directors' maintained by Companies House on its website (www.companieshouse.gov.uk). This has been made available in an attempt to 'name and shame' offenders. In addition, to enforce disqualification orders, the Insolvency Service operates a 'disqualified directors' hotline', encouraging members of the public to name disqualified directors who are blatantly continuing to act despite disqualification orders made against them.

Grounds for disqualification

There are many grounds for disqualification under CDDA 1986, but they normally involve culpable mismanagement. Application for disqualification is made under the relevant section of CDDA 1986 and, depending on which section applies, may be automatic, an outcome of certain defined events, or discretionary:

- **Disqualification for unfitness** (CDDA 1986, s6): Where a company is or has been insolvent, the court is obliged to make a disqualification order against a director, for between two and fifteen years, where it is satisfied that the director's conduct makes him or her 'unfit' to be involved in management of a company. The court will consider the matters set out in Sch 1, Parts I and II to the CDDA 1986 when determining whether there has been a breach of duty (Appendix 12).

For example, in *Official Receiver v Doshi (2001) 2 BCLC 235* a director of an insolvent company was disqualified for 12 years for unfitness resulting from false invoicing and evading VAT. Furthermore, in *Structural Concrete Ltd, ChD (Blackburne J) [2000] 26 LS Gaz R 35* the deliberate policy of withholding crown debts to finance the company's business was considered misconduct for which directors were disqualified for two and five years.

- **Conviction of an indictable offence** (CDDA 1986, s2): The court may make a disqualification order against someone who has been convicted of an indictable offence in connection with the promotion, formation, management or liquidation of a company or with the receivership or management of a company's property. The offence must have some bearing on the management of a company and, where the director is convicted summarily, the maximum period of disqualification is five years, in other cases it is 15 years.

  Such occurrences might involve insider dealing (*R v Goodman [1993] 2 All ER 789*) or carrying on insurance or financial services without the required authorisation.

- **Persistent breaches of statutory obligations** (CDDA 1986, s3): A disqualification order may be made against a person for a maximum of five years for persistent breaches of statutory obligations, such as failure to prepare and submit annual accounts, returns or other documents to the Registrar of Companies.

  For example, in *Secretary of State for Trade and Industry v Ettinger [1993] BCLC 896, CA* two directors were disqualified, one for two years, the other for five, based on their persistent failure to comply with requirements to file annual audited accounts.

- **Fraudulent trading** (CDDA 1986, s4): A disqualification order for a maximum of 15 years may be made against a person who, in the course of winding up a company, is found to be guilty of an offence for fraudulent trading (CA 1985, s458) or has committed some other fraud or breach of duty whilst an officer of the company.

  For example, in *Re Funtime Ltd [2000] 1 BCLC 247* an unfit director of an insolvent company was disqualified for five years for permitting transactions constituting preferences.

- **Conviction of a summary offence** (CDDA 1986, s5): The court may make a disqualification order against someone who has been convicted of a summary offence as a consequence of continuous failure to meet statutory obligations to file returns, accounts or other documents. At least three default orders have to have been made against the person, and the disqualification order will be for a maximum period of five years.

- **Public interest** (CDDA 1986, s8): The Secretary of State has power to apply to the court for a disqualification order where such an order appears to be in the public interest, even where the company is still solvent. This may occur following a report by DTI inspectors or from information or documents obtained under the CA 1985 or FSA 1986. Consideration may be given to Schedule 1 to the CDDA 1986 (see Appendix 12) when determining whether the director's conduct makes him or her 'unfit'. The maximum period for disqualification is 15 years.

  For example, in *Re Looe Fish Ltd [1993] BCLC 1160* investigation by the DTI revealed that a director had used his power to allot shares in the company to keep control of the company. The director was disqualified for $2^1/_2$ years as use of his authority to allot shares in this manner was a clear breach of his duty.

- **Competition infringements** (CDDA 1986, ss9A–9E): The court must make a 'competition disqualification order' against a person where the company of which he is a director commits a breach of competition law and the court considers the director's conduct makes him unfit to be concerned in the management of a company. The maximum period for disqualification is 15 years and a director may face disqualification where he or she had reasonable grounds to suspect a breach of competition law but did nothing about it.

- **Wrongful trading** (CDDA 1986, s10): A disqualification order may be made for a maximum of 15 years against a director of a company in insolvent liquidation where the director is required to make a contribution to the company's assets for insolvent trading under IA 1986 ss213 and 214.

  The Court of Appeal clarified in *Secretary of State for Trade and Industry v Cregan (2002) 1 BCLC 99* that both elements of the 'wrongful trading' test, namely that a company is trading whilst insolvent and there is no reasonable prospect that it will be able to meet creditors' claims, must be present to constitute unfitness for the purposes of disqualification.

Obtaining leave of the court to act (CDDA 1986, s17)

A director who is subject to a disqualification order may apply to the court for leave to act as a director or to be involved in the management of a company. Whether the court grants leave to act depends on the director's behaviour and the circumstances giving rise to the disqualification as well as the overriding need to protect the public interest.

A wealth of cases concerning leave of the court to act continues to develop, a very small sample of which are set out below to illustrate how the court makes its decision:

- *Secretary of State for Trade and Industry v Barnett [1998] 2 BCLC 64* in which it was held that, whilst the director had not acted dishonestly, two of the companies in which he was involved had collapsed at the expense of creditors. It was not considered appropriate for the court to grant leave to act.
- *Re Barings plc [1999] 1 BCLC 262* leave of the court to act as an unpaid non-executive director was granted where fellow directors submitted affidavits to the court stating that they valued the director's advice and expertise in company management. The court decided that the need for the director to act was balanced with the need to protect the public. Leave was granted on the condition that the director continued in a non-executive capacity and did not enter into an employment contract or receive director's fees from the company concerned.
- In *Secretary of State for Trade and Industry v Rosenfield [1999] BCC 413* leave of the court to act was granted as failure to do so may have resulted in serious consequences for employees of the company concerned. In granting leave to act, the court required the production of quarterly accounts and the appointment of a person with financial expertise to the board.
- In *Shuttleworth v Secretary of State for Trade and Industry [2000] BCC 204* the High Court gave leave for a disqualified director to take part in the management of a company in circumstances where the disqualification resulted from inadequate management rather

than dishonesty or a lack of probity, and the new company to which the individual was seeking appointment as a director was unlimited.

Voluntary disqualification undertaking

Provisions contained in the Insolvency Act 2000, ss5–8 permit a director of an insolvent company who recognises and accepts that there are grounds for his or her disqualification to give a voluntary undertaking to the Secretary of State not to act as a director or be involved in the management of a company.

If the Secretary of State considers the director's conduct in relation to the company makes him or her unfit to be involved in management of a company, the director may accept the undertaking if he or she feels that to do so would be in the public interest (CDDA 1986, s7(2A)). Account will be taken of the matters for determining unfitness, detailed in Schedule 1 of the CDDA 1986 (Appendix 12), when the Secretary of State is considering whether to accept the undertaking.

As well as giving a voluntary disqualification undertaking, directors who consider themselves unfit must also provide a 'statement of unfitness', setting out their own admission of events and conduct (clarified in *Secretary of State for Trade and Industry v Davies [2001] All ER (D) 96, (May)* following *Secretary of State for Trade and Industry v Davies All ER (D) 27 (Sept), CA*).

The voluntary undertaking has the same legal effect as a disqualification order but is intended to save time and money. This is particularly important where the company is insolvent and funds are to be recovered from directors for payment to creditors, etc.

A disqualification undertaking may be given for between two and fifteen years.

Ratifying breaches of duty

In certain circumstances the company has power, whether by resolution of the director or members, to ratify a director's breach of duty after the event, for example where:
- shares were allotted for an improper purpose;
- the director failed to disclose his or her interest in a contract;
- the director's personal profit or advantage from a transaction was not disclosed;

- the director's duty of skill and care was not exercised, provided it was not fraudulent;
- the act was outside the company's powers.

However, breaches cannot be ratified where they infringe shareholders' rights, are fraudulent or dishonest, or involve a secret profit being made by a director at the direct expense of the company.

Appendix 1

The Combined Code on Corporate Governance July 2003

CODE OF BEST PRACTICE

SECTION 1 COMPANIES

A.   DIRECTORS

A.1   The Board

Main Principle

Every company should be headed by an effective board, which is collectively responsible for the success of the company.

Supporting Principles

The board's role is to provide entrepreneurial leadership of the company within a framework of prudent and effective controls which enables risk to be assessed and managed. The board should set the company's strategic aims, ensure that the necessary financial and human resources are in place for the company to meet its objectives and review management performance. The board should set the company's values and standards and ensure that its obligations to its shareholders and others are understood and met.

All directors must take decisions objectively in the interests of the company.

As part of their role as members of a unitary board, non-executive directors should constructively challenge and help develop proposals on strategy. Non-executive directors should scrutinise the performance of management in meeting agreed goals and objectives and monitor the reporting of performance. They should satisfy themselves on the integrity of financial information and that financial controls and systems of risk management are robust and defensible. They are responsible for determining appropriate levels of remuneration of executive directors and have a prime role in appointing, and where necessary removing, executive directors, and in succession planning.

Code Provisions

A.1.1   The board should meet sufficiently regularly to discharge its duties effectively. There should be a formal schedule of matters specifically reserved for its decision. The annual report should include a statement of how the board operates, including a high level statement of which types of decisions are to be taken by the board and which are to be delegated to management.

A.1.2   The annual report should identify the chairman, the deputy chairman (where there is one), the chief executive, the senior independent director and the chairmen and members of the nomination, audit and remuneration committees. It should also set out the number of meetings of the board and those committees and individual attendance by directors.

A.1.3   The chairman should hold meetings with the non-executive directors without the executives present. Led by the senior independent director, the non-executive directors should meet without the chairman present at least annually to appraise the chairman's performance (as described in A.6.1) and on such other occasions as are deemed appropriate.

A.1.4 Where directors have concerns which cannot be resolved about the running of the company or a proposed action, they should ensure that their concerns are recorded in the board minutes. On resignation, a non-executive director should provide a written statement to the chairman, for circulation to the board, if they have any such concerns.

A.1.5 The company should arrange appropriate insurance cover in respect of legal action against its directors.

A.2   Chairman and chief executive

Main Principle

There should be a clear division of responsibilities at the head of the company between the running of the board and the executive responsibility for the running of the company's business. No one individual should have unfettered powers of decision.

Supporting Principle

The chairman is responsible for leadership of the board, ensuring its effectiveness on all aspects of its role and setting its agenda. The chairman is also responsible for ensuring that the directors receive accurate, timely and clear information. The chairman should ensure effective communication with shareholders. The chairman should also facilitate the effective contribution of non-executive directors in particular and ensure constructive relations between executive and non-executive directors.

Code Provisions

A.2.1 The roles of chairman and chief executive should not be exercised by the same individual. The division of responsibilities between the chairman and chief executive should be clearly established, set out in writing and agreed by the board.

A.2.2 (5) The chairman should on appointment meet the independence criteria set out in A.3.1 below. A chief executive should not go on to be chairman of the same company. If exceptionally a board decides that a chief executive should become chairman, the board should consult major shareholders in advance and should set out its reasons to shareholders at the time of the appointment and in the next annual report.

A.3.   Board balance and independence

Main Principle

The board should include a balance of executive and non-executive directors (and in particular independent non-executive directors) such that no individual or small group of individuals can dominate the board's decision taking.

Supporting Principles

The board should not be so large as to be unwieldy. The board should be of sufficient size that the balance of skills and experience is appropriate for the requirements of the business and that changes to the board's composition can be managed without undue disruption.

To ensure that power and information are not concentrated in one or two individuals, there should be a strong presence on the board of both executive and non-executive directors.

The value of ensuring that committee membership is refreshed and that undue reliance is not placed on particular individuals should be taken into account in deciding chairmanship and membership of committees. No one other than the committee chairman and members is entitled to be present at a meeting of the nomination, audit or remuneration committee, but others may attend at the invitation of the committee.

Code Provisions

A.3.1   The board should identify in the annual report each non-executive director it considers to be independent. (6) The board should determine whether the director is independent in character and judgement and whether there are relationships or circumstances which are likely to affect, or could appear to affect, the director's judgement. The board should state its reasons if it determines that a director is independent notwithstanding the existence of relationships or circumstances which may appear relevant to its determination, including if the director:

  - has been an employee of the company or group within the last five years;

  - has, or has had within the last three years, a material business relationship with the company either directly, or as a partner, shareholder, director or senior employee of a body that has such a relationship with the company;

  - has received or receives additional remuneration from the company apart from a director's fee, participates in the company's share option or a performance-related pay scheme, or is a member of the company's pension scheme;

  - has close family ties with any of the company's advisers, directors or senior employees;

  - holds cross-directorships or has significant links with other directors through involvement in other companies or bodies;

  - represents a significant shareholder; or

  - has served on the board for more than nine years from the date of their first election.

A.3.2   Except for smaller companies, at least half the board, excluding the chairman, should comprise non-executive directors determined by the board to be independent. A smaller company should have at least two independent non-executive directors.

A.3.3.   The board should appoint one of the independent non-executive directors to be the senior independent director. The senior independent director should be available to shareholders if they have concerns which contact through the normal channels of chairman, chief executive or finance director has failed to resolve or for which such contact is inappropriate.

A.4   Appointments to the Board

Main Principle

There should be a formal, rigorous and transparent procedure for the appointment of new directors to the board.

Supporting Principles

Appointments to the board should be made on merit and against objective criteria. Care should be taken to ensure that appointees have enough time available to devote to the job. This is particularly important in the case of chairmanships.

The board should satisfy itself that plans are in place for orderly succession for appointments to the board and to senior management, so as to maintain an appropriate balance of skills and experience within the company and on the board.

Code Provisions

A.4.1   There should be a nomination committee which should lead the process for board appointments and make recommendations to the board. A majority of members of the nomination committee should be independent non-executive directors. The chairman or an independent non-executive director should chair the committee, but the chairman should not chair the nomination committee when it is dealing with the appointment of a successor to the chairmanship. The nomination committee should make available (8) its terms of reference, explaining its role and the authority delegated to it by the board.

A.4.2   The nomination committee should evaluate the balance of skills, knowledge and experience on the board and, in the light of this evaluation, prepare a description of the role and capabilities required for a particular appointment.

A.4.3   For the appointment of a chairman, the nomination committee should prepare a job specification, including an assessment of the time commitment expected, recognising the need for availability in the event of crises. A chairman's other significant commitments should be disclosed to the board before appointment and included in the annual report. Changes to such commitments should be reported to the board as they arise, and included in the next annual report. No individual should be appointed to a second chairmanship of a FTSE 100 company (9).

A.4.4   The terms and conditions of appointment of non-executive directors should be made available for inspection (10). The letter of appointment should set out the expected time commitment. Non-executive directors should undertake that they will have sufficient time to meet what is expected of them. Their other significant commitments should be disclosed to the board before appointment, with a broad indication of the time involved and the board should be informed of subsequent changes.

A.4.5   The board should not agree to a full time executive director taking on more than one non-executive directorship in a FTSE 100 company nor the chairmanship of such a company.

A.4.6   A separate section of the annual report should describe the work of the nomination committee, including the process it has used in relation to board appointments. An explanation should be given if neither an external search consultancy nor open advertising has been used in the appointment of a chairman or a non-executive director.

A.5   Information and professional development

Main Principle

The board should be supplied in a timely manner with information in a form and of a quality appropriate to enable it to discharge its duties. All directors should receive induction on joining the board and should regularly update and refresh their skills and knowledge.

Supporting Principles

The chairman is responsible for ensuring that the directors receive accurate, timely and clear information. Management has an obligation to provide such information but directors should seek clarification or amplification where necessary.

The chairman should ensure that the directors continually update their skills and the knowledge and familiarity with the company required to fulfil their role both on the board and on board committees. The company should provide the necessary resources for development and updating its directors' knowledge and capabilities.

Under the direction of the chairman, the company secretary's responsibilities include ensuring good information flows within the board and its committees and between senior management and non-executive directors, as well as facilitating induction and assisting with professional development as required.

The company secretary should be responsible for advising the board through the chairman on all governance matters.

Code Provisions

A.5.1   The chairman should ensure that new directors receive a full, formal and tailored induction on joining the board. As part of this, the company should offer to major shareholders the opportunity to meet a new non-executive director.

A.5.2   The board should ensure that directors, especially non-executive directors, have access to independent professional advice at the company's expense where they judge it necessary to discharge their responsibilities as directors. Committees should be provided with sufficient resources to undertake their duties.

A.5.3   All directors should have access to the advice and services of the company secretary, who is responsible to the board for ensuring that board procedures are complied with. Both the appointment and removal of the company secretary should be a matter for the board as a whole.

A.6   Performance evaluation

Main Principle

The board should undertake a formal and rigorous annual evaluation of its own performance and that of its committees and individual directors.

Supporting Principle

Individual evaluation should aim to show whether each director continues to contribute effectively and to demonstrate commitment to the role (including commitment of time for board and committee meetings and any other duties). The chairman should act on the results of the performance evaluation by recognising the strengths and addressing the weaknesses of the board and, where appropriate, proposing new members be appointed to the board or seeking the resignation of directors.

Code Provision

A.6.1   The board should state in the annual report how performance evaluation of the board, its committees and its individual directors has been conducted. The non-executive directors, led by the senior independent director, should be responsible for performance evaluation of the chairman, taking into account the views of executive directors.

A.7 Re-election

Main Principle

All directors should be submitted for re-election at regular intervals, subject to continued satisfactory performance. The board should ensure planned and progressive refreshing of the board.

Code Provisions

A.7.1 All directors should be subject to election by shareholders at the first annual general meeting after their appointment, and to re-election thereafter at intervals of no more than three years. The names of directors submitted for election or re-election should be accompanied by sufficient biographical details and any other relevant information to enable shareholders to take an informed decision on their election.

A.7.2 Non-executive directors should be appointed for specified terms subject to re-election and to Companies Acts provisions relating to the removal of a director. The board should set out to shareholders in the papers accompanying a resolution to elect a non-executive director why they believe an individual should be elected. The chairman should confirm to shareholders when proposing re-election that, following formal performance evaluation, the individual's performance continues to be effective and to demonstrate commitment to the role. Any term beyond six years (e.g. two three-year terms) for a non-executive director should be subject to particularly rigorous review, and should take into account the need for progressive refreshing of the board. Non-executive directors may serve longer than nine years (e.g. three three-year terms), subject to annual re-election. Serving more than nine years could be relevant to the determination of a non-executive director's independence (as set out in provision A.3.1).

B. REMUNERATION

B.1 The Level and Make-up of Remuneration (11)

Main Principles

Levels of remuneration should be sufficient to attract, retain and motivate directors of the quality required to run the company successfully, but a company should avoid paying more than is necessary for this purpose. A significant proportion of executive directors' remuneration should be structured so as to link rewards to corporate and individual performance.

Supporting Principle

The remuneration committee should judge where to position their company relative to other companies. But they should use such comparisons with caution, in view of the risk of an upward ratchet of remuneration levels with no corresponding improvement in performance. They should also be sensitive to pay and employment conditions elsewhere in the group, especially when determining annual salary increases.

Code Provisions

Remuneration policy

B.1.1   The performance-related elements of remuneration should form a significant proportion of the total remuneration package of executive directors and should be designed to align their interests with those of shareholders and to give these directors keen incentives to perform at the highest levels. In designing schemes of performance-related remuneration, the remuneration committee should follow the provisions in Schedule A to this Code.

B.1.2   Executive share options should not be offered at a discount save as permitted by the relevant provisions of the Listing Rules.

B.1.3   Levels of remuneration for non-executive directors should reflect the time commitment and responsibilities of the role. Remuneration for non-executive directors should not include share options. If, exceptionally, options are granted, shareholder approval should be sought in advance and any shares acquired by exercise of the options should be held until at least one year after the non-executive director leaves the board. Holding of share options could be relevant to the determination of a non-executive director's independence (as set out in provision A.3.1).

B.1.4   Where a company releases an executive director to serve as a non-executive director elsewhere, the remuneration report (12) should include a statement as to whether or not the director will retain such earnings and, if so, what the remuneration is.

Service Contracts and Compensation

B.1.5   The remuneration committee should carefully consider what compensation commitments (including pension contributions and all other elements) their directors' terms of appointment would entail in the event of early termination. The aim should be to avoid rewarding poor performance. They should take a robust line on reducing compensation to reflect departing directors' obligations to mitigate loss.

B.1.6   Notice or contract periods should be set at one year or less. If it is necessary to offer longer notice or contract periods to new directors recruited from outside, such periods should reduce to one year or less after the initial period.

B.2   Procedure

Main Principle

There should be a formal and transparent procedure for developing policy on executive remuneration and for fixing the remuneration packages of individual directors. No director should be involved in deciding his or her own remuneration.

Supporting Principles

The remuneration committee should consult the chairman and/or chief executive about their proposals relating to the remuneration of other executive directors. The remuneration committee should also be responsible for appointing any consultants in respect of executive director remuneration. Where executive directors or senior management are involved in advising or supporting the remuneration committee, care should be taken to recognise and avoid conflicts of interest. The chairman of the board should ensure that the company maintains contact as required with its principal shareholders about remuneration in the same way as for other matters.

Code Provisions

B.2.1   The board should establish a remuneration committee of at least three, or in the case of smaller companies (13) two, members, who should all be independent non-executive directors. The remuneration committee should make available (14) its terms of reference, explaining its role and the authority delegated to it by the board. Where remuneration consultants are appointed, a statement should be made available (15) of whether they have any other connection with the company.

B.2.2   The remuneration committee should have delegated responsibility for setting remuneration for all executive directors and the chairman, including pension rights and any compensation payments. The committee should also recommend and monitor the level and structure of remuneration for senior management. The definition of 'senior management' for this purpose should be determined by the board but should normally include the first layer of management below board level.

B.2.3   The board itself or, where required by the Articles of Association, the shareholders should determine the remuneration of the non-executive directors within the limits set in the Articles of Association. Where permitted by the Articles, the board may however delegate this responsibility to a committee, which might include the chief executive.

B.2.4   Shareholders should be invited specifically to approve all new long-term incentive schemes (as defined in the Listing rules) and significant changes to existing schemes, save in the circumstances permitted by the Listing Rules.

C.   ACCOUNTABILITY AND AUDIT

C.1   Financial Reporting

Main Principle

The board should present a balanced and understandable assessment of the company's position and prospects.

Supporting Principle

The board's responsibility to present a balanced and understandable assessment extends to interim and other price-sensitive public reports and reports to regulators as well as to information required to be presented by statutory requirements.

Code Provisions

C.1.1   The directors should explain in the annual report their responsibility for preparing the accounts and there should be a statement by the auditors about their reporting responsibilities.

C.1.2   The directors should report that the business is a going concern, with supporting assumptions or qualifications as necessary.

C.2.   Internal Control (16)

Main Principle

The board should maintain a sound system of internal control to safeguard shareholders' investment and the company's assets.

Code Provision

C.2.1   The board should, at least annually, conduct a review of the effectiveness of the group's system of internal controls and should report to shareholders that they have done so. The review should cover all material controls, including financial, operational and compliance controls and risk management systems.

C.3   Audit Committee and Auditors (17)

Main Principle

The board should establish formal and transparent arrangements for considering how they should apply the financial reporting and internal control principles and for maintaining an appropriate relationship with the company's auditors.

Code Provisions

C.3.1   The board should establish an audit committee of at least three, or in the case of smaller companies (18) two, members, who should all be independent non-executive directors. The board should satisfy itself that at least one member of the audit committee has recent and relevant financial experience.

C.3.2   The main role and responsibilities of the audit committee should be set out in written terms of reference and should include:

– to monitor the integrity of the financial statements of the company, and any formal announcements relating to the company's financial performance, reviewing significant financial reporting judgements contained in them;

– to review the company's internal financial controls and, unless expressly addressed by a separate board risk committee composed of independent directors, or by the board itself, to review the company's internal control and risk management systems;

– to monitor and review the effectiveness of the company's internal audit function;

– to make recommendations to the board, for it to put to the shareholders for their approval in general meeting, in relation to the appointment, re-appointment and removal of the external auditor and to approve the remuneration and terms of engagement of the external auditor;

– to review and monitor the external auditor's independence and objectivity and the effectiveness of the audit process, taking into consideration relevant UK professional and regulatory requirements;

– to develop and implement policy on the engagement of the external auditor to supply non-audit services, taking into account relevant ethical guidance regarding the provision of non-audit services by the external audit firm; and to report to the board, identifying any matters in respect of which it considers that action or improvement is needed and making recommendations as to the steps to be taken.

C.3.3   The terms of reference of the audit committee, including its role and the authority delegated to it by the board, should be made available. (19) A separate section of the annual report should describe the work of the committee in discharging those responsibilities.

C.3.4   The audit committee should review arrangements by which staff of the company may, in confidence, raise concerns about possible improprieties in matters of financial reporting or other matters. The audit committee's objective should be to ensure that arrangements are in place for the proportionate and independent investigation of such matters and for appropriate follow-up action.

C.3.5   The audit committee should monitor and review the effectiveness of the internal audit activities. Where there is no internal audit function, the audit committee should consider annually whether there is a need for an internal audit function and make a recommendation to the board, and the reasons for the absence of such a function should be explained in the relevant section of the annual report.

C.3.6   The audit committee should have primary responsibility for making a recommendation on the appointment, reappointment and removal of the external auditors. If the board does not accept the audit committee's recommendation, it should include in the annual report, and in any papers recommending appointment or re-appointment, a statement from the audit committee explaining the recommendation and should set out reasons why the board has taken a different position.

C.3.7   The annual report should explain to shareholders how, if the auditor provides non-audit services, auditor objectivity and independence is safeguarded.

D.   RELATIONS WITH SHAREHOLDERS

D.1.   Dialogue with Institutional Shareholders

Main Principle

There should be a dialogue with shareholders based on the mutual understanding of objectives. The board as a whole has responsibility for ensuring that a satisfactory dialogue with shareholders takes place. (20)

Supporting Principles

Whilst recognising that most shareholder contact is with the chief executive and finance director, the chairman (and the senior independent director and other directors as appropriate) should maintain sufficient contact with major shareholders to understand their issues and concerns. The board should keep in touch with shareholder opinion in whatever ways are most practical and efficient.

Code Provisions

D.1.1   The chairman should ensure that the views of shareholders are communicated to the board as a whole. The chairman should discuss governance and strategy with major shareholders. Non-executive directors should be offered the opportunity to attend meetings with major shareholders and should expect to attend them if requested by major shareholders. The senior independent director should attend sufficient meetings with a range of major shareholders to listen to their views in order to help develop a balanced understanding of the issues and concerns of major shareholders.

D.1.2   The board should state in the annual report the steps they have taken to ensure that the members of the board, and in particular the non-executive directors, develop an understanding of the views of major shareholders about their company, for example through direct face-to-face contact, analysts' or brokers' briefings and surveys of shareholders opinion.

D.2   **Constructive Use of the AGM**

Main Principle

The board should use the AGM to communicate with Investors and to encourage their participation.

Code Provisions

D.2.1   The company should count all proxy votes and, except where a poll is called, should indicate the level of proxies lodged on each resolution, and the balance for and against the resolution and the number of abstentions, after it has been dealt with on a show of hands. The company should ensure that votes cast are properly received and recorded.

D.2.2   The company should propose a separate resolution at the AGM on each substantially separate issue and should in particular propose a resolution at the AGM relating to the report and accounts.

D.2.3   The chairman should arrange for the chairmen of the audit, remuneration and nomination committee to be available to answer questions at the AGM and for all directors to attend.

D.2.4   The company should arrange for the Notice of the AGM and related papers to be sent to shareholders at least 20 working days before the meeting.

SECTION 2 INSTITUTIONAL SHAREHOLDERS

E.   INSTITUTIONAL SHAREHOLDERS (21)

E.1   Dialogue with companies

Main Principle

Institutional shareholders should enter into a dialogue with companies based on the mutual understanding of objectives.

Supporting Principles

Institutional shareholders should apply the principles set out in the Institutional Shareholders' Committee's 'The Responsibilities of Institutional Shareholders and Agents – Statement of Principles' (22), which should be reflected in fund manager contracts.

E.2.   Evaluation of Governance Disclosures

Main Principle

When evaluating companies' governance arrangements, particularly those relating to board structure and composition, institutional shareholders should give due weight to all relevant factors drawn to their attention.

Supporting Principle

Institutional shareholders should consider carefully explanations given for departure from this Code and make reasoned judgements in each case. They should given an explanation to the company, in writing where appropriate, and be prepared to enter a dialogue if they do not accept the company's position. They should avoid a box-ticking approach to assessing a company's corporate governance. They should bear in mind in particular the size and complexity of the company and the nature of the risks and challenges it faces.

E.3   Shareholder Voting

Main Principle

Institutional shareholders have a responsibility to make considered use of their votes.

Supporting Principles

Institutional shareholders should take steps to ensure their voting intentions are being translated into practice.

Institutional shareholders should, on request, make available to their clients information on the proportion of resolutions on which votes were cast and non-discretionary proxies lodged.

Major shareholders should attend AGMs where appropriate and practicable. Companies and registrars should facilitate this.

Appendix 2

Turnbull Report: Internal Control – Guidance for Directors on the Combined Code

© The Institute of Chartered Accountants in England and Wales.

Reproduced with kind permission of the Institute of Chartered Accountants in England and Wales.

Introduction

Internal control requirements of the Combined Code

1. When the Combined Code of the Committee on Corporate Governance (the Code) was published, the Institute of Chartered Accountants in England & Wales agreed with the London Stock Exchange that it would provide guidance to assist listed companies to implement the requirements in the Code relating to internal control.

2. Principle D.2 of the Code states that 'The board should maintain a sound system of internal control to safeguard shareholders' investment and the company's assets'.

3. Provision D.2.1 states that 'The directors should, at least annually, conduct a review of the effectiveness of the group's system of internal control and should report to shareholders that they have done so. The review should cover all controls, including financial, operational and compliance controls and risk management'.

4. Provision D.2.2 states that 'Companies which do not have an internal audit function should from time to time review the need for one'.

5. Paragraph 12.43A of the London Stock Exchange Listing Rules states that 'in the case of a company incorporated in the United Kingdom, the following additional items must be included in its annual report and accounts:

   (a) a narrative statement of how it has applied the principles set out in Section 1 of the Combined Code, providing explanation which enables its shareholders to evaluate how the principles have been applied;

   (b) a statement as to whether or not it has complied throughout the accounting period with the Code provisions set out in Section 1 of the Combined Code. A company that has not complied with the Code provisions, or complied with only some of the Code provisions or (in the case of provisions whose requirements are of a continuing nature) complied for only part of an accounting period, must specify the Code provisions with which it has not complied, and (where relevant) for what part of the period such non-compliance continued, and give reasons for any non-compliance'.

6. The Preamble to the Code, which is appended to the Listing Rules, makes it clear that there is no prescribed form or content for the statement setting out how the various principles in the Code have been applied. The intention is that companies should have a free hand to explain their governance policies in the light of the principles, including any special circumstances which have led to them adopting a particular approach.

7. The guidance in this document should be followed by boards of listed companies in:

  ı assessing how the company has applied Code principle D.2;

  ı implementing the requirements of Code provisions D.2.1 and D.2.2; and

  ı reporting on these matters to shareholders in the annual report and accounts.

Objectives of the guidance

8. This guidance is intended to:

  ı reflect sound business practice whereby internal control is embedded in the business processes by which a company pursues its objectives;

  ı remain relevant over time in the continually evolving business environment; and

  ı enable each company to apply it in a manner which takes account of its particular circumstances.

  The guidance requires directors to exercise judgement in reviewing how the company has implemented the requirements of the Code relating to internal control and reporting to shareholders thereon.

9. The guidance is based on the adoption by a company's board of a risk-based approach to establishing a sound system of internal control and reviewing its effectiveness. This should be incorporated by the company within its normal management and governance processes. It should not be treated as a separate exercise undertaken to meet regulatory requirements.

The importance of internal control and risk management

10. A company's system of internal control has a key role in the management of risks that are significant to the fulfilment of its business objectives. A sound system of internal control contributes to safeguarding the shareholders' investment and the company's assets.

11. Internal control (as referred to in paragraph 20) facilitates the effectiveness and efficiency of operations, helps ensure the reliability of internal and external reporting and assists compliance with laws and regulations.

12. Effective financial controls, including the maintenance of proper accounting records, are an important element of internal control. They help ensure that the company is not unnecessarily exposed to avoidable financial risks and that financial information used within the business and for publication is reliable. They also contribute to the safeguarding of assets, including the prevention and detection of fraud.

13. A company's objectives, its internal organisation and the environment in which it operates are continually evolving and, as a result, the risks it faces are continually changing. A sound system of internal control therefore depends on a thorough and regular evaluation of the nature and extent of the risks to which the company is exposed. Since profits are, in part, the reward for successful risk-taking in business, the purpose of internal control is to help manage and control risk appropriately rather than to eliminate it.

Groups of companies

14. Throughout this guidance, where reference is made to 'company' it should be taken, where applicable, as referring to the group of which the reporting company is the parent company. For groups of companies, the review of effectiveness of internal control and the report to the shareholders should be from the perspective of the group as a whole.

The Appendix

15. The Appendix to this document contains questions which boards may wish to consider in applying this guidance.

Maintaining a sound system of internal control

Responsibilities

16. The board of directors is responsible for the company's system of internal control. It should set appropriate policies on internal control and seek regular assurance that will enable it to satisfy itself that the system is functioning effectively. The board must further ensure that the system of internal control is effective in managing risks in the manner which it has approved.

17. In determining its policies with regard to internal control, and thereby assessing what constitutes a sound system of internal control in the particular circumstances of the company, the board's deliberations should include consideration of the following factors:

ı the nature and extent of the risks facing the company;

ı the extent and categories of risk which it regards as acceptable for the company to bear;

ı the likelihood of the risks concerned materialising;

ı the company's ability to reduce the incidence and impact on the business of risks that do materialise; and ι   the costs of operating particular controls relative to the benefit thereby obtained in managing the related risks.

18. It is the role of management to implement board policies on risk and control. In fulfilling its responsibilities, management should identify and evaluate the risks faced by the company for consideration by the board and design, operate and monitor a suitable system of internal control which implements the policies adopted by the board.

19. All employees have some responsibility for internal control as part of their accountability for achieving objectives. They, collectively, should have the necessary knowledge, skills, information and authority to establish, operate and monitor the system of internal control. This will require an understanding of the company, its objectives, the industries and markets in which it operates, and the risks it faces.

20. An internal control system encompasses the policies, processes, tasks, behaviours and other aspects of a company that, taken together:

ι   facilitate its effective and efficient operation by enabling it to respond appropriately to significant business, operational, financial, compliance and other risks to achieving the company's objectives. This includes the safeguarding of assets from inappropriate use or from loss and fraud, and ensuring that liabilities are identified and managed;

ι   help ensure the quality of internal and external reporting. This requires the maintenance of proper records and processes that generate a flow of timely, relevant and reliable information from within and outside the organisation;

ι   help ensure compliance with applicable laws and regulations, and also with internal policies with respect to the conduct of business.

21. A company's system of internal control will reflect its control environment which encompasses its organisational structure. The system will include:

ι   control activities;

ι   information and communications processes; and

ι   processes for monitoring the continuing effectiveness of the system of internal control.

22. The system of internal control should:

ι   be embedded in the operations of the company and form part of its culture;

ι   be capable of responding quickly to evolving risks to the business arising from factors within the company and to changes in the business environment; and

ι   include procedures for reporting immediately to appropriate levels of management any significant control failings or weaknesses that are identified together with details of corrective action being undertaken.

137

23. A sound system of internal control reduces, but cannot eliminate, the possibility of poor judgement in decision-making; human error; control processes being deliberately circumvented by employees and others; management overriding controls; and the occurrence of unforeseeable circumstances.

24. A sound system of internal control therefore provides reasonable, but not absolute, assurance that a company will not be hindered in achieving its business objectives, or in the orderly and legitimate conduct of its business, by circumstances which may reasonably be foreseen. A system of internal control cannot, however, provide protection with certainty against a company failing to meet its business objectives or all material errors, losses, fraud, or breaches of laws or regulations.

Reviewing the effectiveness of internal control

Responsibilities

25. Reviewing the effectiveness of internal control is an essential part of the board's responsibilities. The board will need to form its own view on effectiveness after due and careful enquiry based on the information and assurances provided to it. Management is accountable to the board for monitoring the system of internal control and for providing assurance to the board that it has done so.

26. The role of board committees in the review process, including that of the audit committee, is for the board to decide and will depend upon factors such as the size and composition of the board; the scale, diversity and complexity of the company's operations; and the nature of the significant risks that the company faces. To the extent that designated board committees carry out, on behalf of the board, tasks that are attributed in this guidance document to the board, the results of the relevant committees' work should be reported to, and considered by, the board. The board takes responsibility for the disclosures on internal control in the annual report and accounts.

The process for reviewing effectiveness

27. Effective monitoring on a continuous basis is an essential component of a sound system of internal control. The board cannot, however, rely solely on the embedded monitoring processes within the company to discharge its responsibilities. It should regularly receive and review reports on internal control. In addition, the board should undertake an annual assessment for the purposes of making its public statement on internal control to ensure that it has considered all significant aspects of internal control for the company for the year under review and up to the date of approval of the annual report and accounts.

28. The reference to 'all controls' in Code Provision D.2.1 should not be taken to mean that the effectiveness of every internal control (including controls designed to manage immaterial risks) should be subject to review by the board. Rather it means that, for the purposes of this guidance, internal controls considered by the board should include all types of controls including those of an operational and compliance nature, as well as internal financial controls.

29. The board should define the process to be adopted for its review of the effectiveness of internal control. This should encompass both the scope and frequency of the reports it receives and reviews during the year, and also the process for its annual assessment, such that it will be provided with sound, appropriately documented, support for its statement on internal control in the company's annual report and accounts.

30. The reports from management to the board should, in relation to the areas covered by them, provide a balanced assessment of the significant risks and the effectiveness of the system of internal control in managing those risks. Any significant control failings or weaknesses identified should be discussed in the reports, including the impact that they have had, could have had, or may have, on the company and the actions being taken to rectify them. It is essential that there be openness of communication by management with the board on matters relating to risk and control.

31. When reviewing reports during the year, the board should:

    i   consider what are the significant risks and assess how they have been identified, evaluated and managed;

    i   assess the effectiveness of the related system of internal control in managing the significant risks, having regard, in particular, to any significant failings or weaknesses in internal control that have been reported;

    i   consider whether necessary actions are being taken promptly to remedy any significant failings or weaknesses; and

    i   consider whether the findings indicate a need for more extensive monitoring of the system of internal control.

32. Additionally, the board should undertake an annual assessment for the purpose of making its public statement on internal control. The assessment should consider issues dealt with in reports reviewed by it during the year together with any additional information necessary to ensure that the board has taken account of all significant aspects of internal control for the company for the year under review and up to the date of approval of the annual report and accounts.

33. The board's annual assessment should, in particular, consider:

    i   the changes since the last annual assessment in the nature and extent of significant risks, and the company's ability to respond to changes in its business and the external environment;

    i   the scope and quality of management's ongoing monitoring of risks and of the system of internal control, and, where applicable, the work of its internal audit function and other providers of assurance;

ı the extent and frequency of the communication of the results of the monitoring to the board (or board committee(s)) which enables it to build up a cumulative assessment of the state of control in the company and the effectiveness with which risk is being managed;

ı the incidence of significant control failings or weaknesses that have been identified at any time during the period and the extent to which they have resulted in unforeseen outcomes or contingencies that have had, could have had, or may in the future have, a material impact on the company's financial performance or condition; and

ı the effectiveness of the company's public reporting processes.

34. Should the board become aware at any time of a significant failing or weakness in internal control, it should determine how the failing or weakness arose and re-assess the effectiveness of management's ongoing processes for designing, operating and monitoring the system of internal control.

The board's statement on internal control

35. In its narrative statement of how the company has applied Code principle D.2, the board should, as a minimum, disclose that there is an ongoing process for identifying, evaluating and managing the significant risks faced by the company, that it has been in place for the year under review and up to the date of approval of the annual report and accounts, that it is regularly reviewed by the board and accords with the guidance in this document.

36. The board may wish to provide additional information in the annual report and accounts to assist understanding of the company's risk management processes and system of internal control.

37. The disclosures relating to the application of principle D.2 should include an acknowledgement by the board that it is responsible for the company's system of internal control and for reviewing its effectiveness. It should also explain that such a system is designed to manage rather than eliminate the risk of failure to achieve business objectives, and can only provide reasonable and not absolute assurance against material misstatement or loss.

38. In relation to Code provision D.2.1, the board should summarise the process it (where applicable, through its committees) has applied in reviewing the effectiveness of the system of internal control. It should also disclose the process it has applied to deal with material internal control aspects of any significant problems disclosed in the annual report and accounts.

39. Where a board cannot make one or more of the disclosures in paragraphs 35 and 38, it should state this fact and provide an explanation. The Listing Rules require the board to disclose if it has failed to conduct a review of the effectiveness of the company's system of internal control.

40. The board should ensure that its disclosures provide meaningful, high-level information and do not give a misleading impression.

41. Where material joint ventures and associates have not been dealt with as part of the group for the purposes of applying this guidance, this should be disclosed.

Internal audit

42. Provision D.2.2 of the Code states that companies which do not have an internal audit function should from time to time review the need for one.

43. The need for an internal audit function will vary depending on company-specific factors including the scale, diversity and complexity of the company's activities and the number of employees, as well as cost/benefit considerations. Senior management and the board may desire objective assurance and advice on risk and control. An adequately resourced internal audit function (or its equivalent where, for example, a third party is contracted to perform some or all of the work concerned) may provide such assurance and advice. There may be other functions within the company that also provide assurance and advice covering specialist areas such as health and safety, regulatory and legal compliance and environmental issues.

44. In the absence of an internal audit function, management needs to apply other monitoring processes in order to assure itself and the board that the system of internal control is functioning as intended. In these circumstances, the board will need to assess whether such processes provide sufficient and objective assurance.

45. When undertaking its assessment of the need for an internal audit function, the board should also consider whether there are any trends or current factors relevant to the company's activities, markets or other aspects of its external environment, that have increased, or are expected to increase, the risks faced by the company. Such an increase in risk may also arise from internal factors such as organisational restructuring or from changes in reporting processes or underlying information systems. Other matters to be taken into account may include adverse trends evident from the monitoring of internal control systems or an increased incidence of unexpected occurrences.

46. The board of a company that does not have an internal audit function should assess the need for such a function annually having regard to the factors referred to in paragraphs 43 and 45 above. Where there is an internal audit function, the board should annually review its scope of work, authority and resources, again having regard to those factors.

47. If the company does not have an internal audit function and the board has not reviewed the need for one, the Listing Rules require the board to disclose these facts.

Appendix

Assessing the effectiveness of the company's risk and control processes

Some questions which the board may wish to consider and discuss with management when regularly reviewing reports on internal control and carrying out its annual assessment are set out below. The questions are not intended to be exhaustive and will need to be tailored to the particular circumstances of the company.

This Appendix should be read in conjunction with the guidance set out in this document.

1. Risk assessment
   : Does the company have clear objectives and have they been communicated so as to provide effective direction to employees on risk assessment and control issues? For example, do objectives and related plans include measurable performance targets and indicators?

   : Are the significant internal and external operational, financial, compliance and other risks identified and assessed on an ongoing basis? (Significant risks may, for example, include those related to market, credit, liquidity, technological, legal, health, safety and environmental, reputation, and business probity issues.)

   : Is there a clear understanding by management and others within the company of what risks are acceptable to the board?

2. Control environment and control activities
   : Does the board have clear strategies for dealing with the significant risks that have been identified? Is there a policy on how to manage these risks?

   : Do the company's culture, code of conduct, human resource policies and performance reward systems support the business objectives and risk management and internal control system?

   : Does senior management demonstrate, through its actions as well as its policies, the necessary commitment to competence, integrity and fostering a climate of trust within the company?

   : Are authority, responsibility and accountability defined clearly such that decisions are made and actions taken by the appropriate people? Are the decisions and actions of different parts of the company appropriately co-ordinated?

   : Does the company communicate to its employees what is expected of them and the scope of their freedom to act? This may apply to areas such as customer relations; service levels for both internal and outsourced activities; health, safety and environmental protection; security of tangible and intangible assets; business continuity issues; expenditure matters; accounting; and financial and other reporting.

    ı   Do people in the company (and in its providers of outsourced services) have the knowledge, skills and tools to support the achievement of the company's objectives and to manage effectively risks to their achievement?

    ı   How are processes/controls adjusted to reflect new or changing risks, or operational deficiencies?

3. Information and communication

    ı   Do management and the board receive timely, relevant and reliable reports on progress against business objectives and the related risks that provide them with the information, from inside and outside the company, needed for decision-making and management review purposes? This could include performance reports and indicators of change, together with qualitative information such as on customer satisfaction, employee attitudes etc.

    ı   Are information needs and related information systems reassessed as objectives and related risks change or as reporting deficiencies are identified?

    ı   Are periodic reporting procedures, including half-yearly and annual reporting, effective in communicating a balanced and understandable account of the company's position and prospects?

    ı   Are there established channels of communication for individuals to report suspected breaches of laws or regulations or other improprieties?

4. Monitoring

    ı   Are there ongoing processes embedded within the company's overall business operations, and addressed by senior management, which monitor the effective application of the policies, processes and activities related to internal control and risk management? (Such processes may include control self-assessment, confirmation by personnel of compliance with policies and codes of conduct, internal audit reviews or other management reviews).

    ı   Do these processes monitor the company's ability to re-evaluate risks and adjust controls effectively in response to changes in its objectives, its business, and its external environment?

    ı   Are there effective follow-up procedures to ensure that appropriate change or action occurs in response to changes in risk and control assessments?

    ı   Is there appropriate communication to the board (or board committees) on the effectiveness of the ongoing monitoring processes on risk and control matters? This should include reporting any significant failings or weaknesses on a timely basis.

    ı   Are there specific arrangements for management monitoring and reporting to the board on risk and control matters of particular importance? These could include, for example, actual or suspected fraud and other illegal or irregular acts, or matters that could adversely affect the company's reputation or financial position?

Appendix 3

Directors' interests in shares

Included for disclosure

(i) An interest as a beneficiary under a trust (Sch 13, para 2) and an interest where shares are held by a personal equity plan (PEP) of which the director is the beneficial owner.

(ii) Joint interests (each notifiable) (Sch 13, para 7).

(iii) An interest arising from a contract for the purchase of shares or debentures (Sch 13, para 3).

(iv) An entitlement to exercise any right conferred by the holding of shares or debentures (except as holder of a proxy for a specified meeting) (Sch 13, para 3).

(v) A right to call for delivery of shares or debentures, a right to acquire an interest and an obligation to take an interest in shares or debentures (Sch 13, para 6). A right to subscribe does not constitute an interest for these purposes (Sch 13, para 6), but must be disclosed in its own right.

Excluded from disclosure

(i) A person holding as a bare trustee or custodian trustee* (Sch 13, para 10).

(ii) Interests arising as a trustee or personal representative where the Public Trustee is also a trustee or personal representative (Companies (Disclosure of Directors' Interests) (Exceptions) Regulation 1995 SI 1985/802).

(iii) A remainder interest in trust property, so long as the life interest subsists (Sch 13, para 9).

(iv) Interests of a director of a reporting company, that is a wholly-owned subsidiary, and the director is also the director of the parent company which will report the interest (SI 1985/802).

(v) Where a company is a wholly-owned subsidiary of a company incorporated outside Great Britain, interests in any group companies incorporated outside Great Britain (SI 1985/802).

(vi) An interest acquired through another company, if that company is interested and:
  - that company or its directors are accustomed to act in accordance with the instructions of the notifying director; or
  - the notifying director controls one third of the voting power in that company (Sch 13, para 4).

(vi) Interests in shares arising solely on account of a limitation in the Memorandum or Articles of Association on a person's rights of disposal of shares (SI 1985/802).

(vii) Interests in shares or debentures of a society registered under the Industrial and Provident Societies Act 1965 (SI 1985/802).

(viii) Interests as a trustee or beneficiary of an approved superannuation fund or retirement benefit scheme (SI 1985/802).

* Bare trustee: a trustee whose only duty is to convey the assets to, or by the direction of, the beneficiaries and has no beneficial interest (i.e. as a nominee).

* Custodian trustee: a trustee in whose name assets have been vested but who has no powers of administration and is bound to act in accordance with the directions of the managing trustees, for example a bank that holds the assets of a unit trust.

Appendix 4

Statutory forms and filing periods

Companies registered in England and Wales

Form number	Description	Filing period
6	Notice of application to the court for cancellation of alteration to the objects of a company	15 days of notice
10 (plus continuation)	Statement of first directors and secretary and intended situation of Registered Office	Required for incorporation
12	Statutory Declaration of compliance with requirements on application for registration of a company	Required for incorporation
30(5)a	Declaration on application for the registration of a company exempt from the requirement to use the word 'Limited' or 'Cyfyngedig'	With Form 10
30(5)(b)	Declaration on application for registration under s680, CA 1985 of a company exempt from the requirement to use the word 'Limited' or 'Cyfyngedig'	With Form 630(a)
30(5)(c)	Declaration on change of name omitting 'Limited ' or 'Cyfyngedig'	With change of name resolution
43(3)	Application by a private company for re-registration as a public company	15 days
43(3)(e)	Declaration of compliance with the requirements by a private company for re-registration as a public company	15 days
49(1) (plus continuation)	Application by a limited company to be re-registered as unlimited	15 days
49(8)(a) (plus continuation)	Members' assent to company being re-registered as unlimited	15 days
49(8)(b)	Form of statutory declaration by directors as to members' assent to re-registration of a company as unlimited	15 days
51	Application by an unlimited company to be re-registered as limited	15 days
53	Application by a public company for re-registration as a private company	After 28 days
54	Notice of application made to the court for the cancellation of a special resolution regarding re-registration	On notice
88(2)	Return of allotment of shares	1 month

88(3)	Particulars of a contract relating to shares allotted as fully or partly paid up otherwise than in cash	1 month
97	Statement of the amount or rate per cent of any commission payable in connection with the subscription of shares	Before payment
117	Application by a public company for a certificate to commence business with a Statutory Declaration	No limit but application must be made before the company is permitted to commence trading
122	Notice of consolidation, division, sub-division, redemption or cancellation of shares or conversion, re-conversion of shares into stock	1 month
123	Notice of increase in nominal capital	15 days
128(1)	Statement of rights attached to allotted shares	1 month
128(3)	Statement of particulars of variation of rights attached to shares	1 month
128(4)	Notice of assignment of name or new name to any class of shares	1 month
129(1)	Statement by a company without share capital of rights attached to newly created class of members	1 month
129(2)	Statement by a company without share capital of particulars of a variation of members' class rights	1 month
129(3)	Notice by a company without share capital of assignment of a name or other designation to a class of members	1 month
139	Application by a public company for re-registration as a private company following a court order reducing capital	15 days or as directed by court
147	Application by a public company for re-registration as a private company following cancellation of shares and reduction of nominal value of issued capital	15 days
155(6)(a)	Declaration in relation to assistance for the acquisition of shares	15 days
155(6)(b)	Declaration by the directors of a holding company in relation to assistance for the acquisition of shares	15 days
157	Notice of application made to the court for the cancellation of a Special Resolution regarding financial assistance for the acquisition of shares	On notice

169	Return by a company purchasing its own shares	28 days
173	Declaration in relation to the redemption or purchase of shares out of capital	15 days
176	Notice of application to the court for the cancellation of a resolution for the redemption or purchase of shares out of capital	On notice
190	Notice of place where a register of holders of debentures or a duplicate is kept or of any change in that place	On change of address
190(a)	Notice of place for inspection of a register of holders of debentures which is kept in a non-legible form or of any change in that place	On change of address
225	Notice of change of accounting reference date	At any time before the period for filing accounts has expired
244	Notice of claim to extension of period allowed for laying and delivering accounts – overseas business or interest	Before end of filing period to be extended
266(1)	Notice of intention to carry on business as an investment company	Prior to commencement of investment business
266(3)	Notice that a company no longer wishes to be an investment company	On cessation
287	Notice of change in situation of Registered Office	Change takes effect on delivery
288a	Appointment of director/secretary	14 days
288b	Resignation of director/secretary	14 days
288c	Change of particulars	14 days
318	Notice of location of copies of directors' service contracts and memoranda, or of any change in location	14 days
325	Notice of location of register of directors' interests in shares, etc. or of any change in location	14 days
325(a)	Notice of place for inspection of register of directors' interests in shares, etc. which is kept in a non-legible form or of any change in location	14 days
353	Notice of location of register of members or of any change in location	14 days
353(a)	Notice of place for inspection of a register of members that is kept in a non-legible form or of any change in location	14 days

362	Notice of location of overseas branch register, of any change in location or of discontinuance of any such register	14 days
362(a)	Notice of place for inspection of an overseas branch register which is kept in a non-legible form or of any change in location	14 days
363a (plus continuation)	Company's annual return	28 days
363a Sch	List of past and present members	28 days
363b	Annual return of company	28 days
363s	Company's annual return (shuttle return issued by Companies House)	28 days
391	Notice of a resolution to remove an auditor	14 days
395 (plus continuation)	Particulars of mortgage or charge	21 days
397	Particulars for the registration of a charge to secure a series of debentures	21 days
397(a)	Particulars of an issue of secured debentures in a series	21 days
398	Certificate of registration in Scotland or Northern Ireland of a charge comprising property situated there	21 days
400	Particulars of a mortgage or charge subject to which property has been acquired	21 days
403(a)	Declaration of satisfaction in full or in part of mortgage or charge	–
403(b)	Declaration that part of the property or undertaking charged (a) has been released from the charge or (b) no longer forms part of the company property or undertaking	–
405(1)	Notice of appointment of receiver or manager	7 days
405(2)	Notice of ceasing to act as receiver or manager	7 days
419(a)	Application for registration of a memorandum of satisfaction in full or in part of a registered charge	–
429(4)	Notice to non-assenting shareholders	7 days
429(dec)	Statutory declaration relating to a notice to non-assenting shareholders	–
430a	Notice to non-assenting shareholders	–
600	Notice of appointment of liquidator re voluntary winding up (members or creditors)	14 days
600(a)	Notice of appointment of liquidator re voluntary winding up (members or creditors)	14 days (send to The London Gazette Office)

652(a)	Application for striking off	–
652(c)	Withdrawal of application for striking off	–
680(a)	Application by a joint stock company for registration under Part XXII of CA 1985 and declaration and related statements	Required for registration
680(b)	Application by a company which is not a joint stock company for registration under Part XXII CA 1985 and declaration and related statements	Required for registration
684	Registration under Part XXII CA 1985 giving list of members in existing joint stock company	Required for registration
685	Application by a joint stock company for registration as a public company; Statutory Declaration that conditions satisfied	Required for registration
686	Registration under Part XXII CA 1985 Statutory Declaration verifying list of members	Required for registration

Overseas companies

Form number	Description	Filing period
691	Return and declaration delivered for registration by an overseas company	1 month of establishing business in UK
692(1)(a)	Return of alteration in the charter statutes of an overseas company	21 days
692(1)(b) (plus continuation)	Return of alteration in the directors or secretary of an overseas company or in their particulars	21 days
692(1)(c)	Return of alteration in the names or addresses of persons resident in Great Britain authorised to accept service on behalf of an overseas company	21 days
692(2)	Return of change in the corporate name of an overseas company	21 days
694(4)(a)	Statement of name other than corporate name under which an overseas company proposes to carry on business in Great Britain	On change of name
694(4)(b)	Statement of name other than corporate name under which an overseas company proposes to carry on business in Great Britain in substitution for name previously registered	On change of name
695A(3)	Notice of closure of branch of an overseas company	–
701(a)	Notice of accounting reference date by an overseas company	As 225

703P(1)	Return by an overseas company that company is being wound up	14 days from date of winding up
703P(3)	Notice of appointment of a liquidator of an overseas company	14 days from date of winding up
703P(5)	Notice by a liquidator of an overseas company concerning the termination of liquidation of the company	14 days
703Q(1)	Return by an overseas company which becomes subject to insolvency proceedings	14 days
703Q(2)	Return by an overseas company on cessation of insolvency proceedings	14 days
BR1	Return delivered for registration of a branch of an overseas company	Within 1 month of establishing a branch
BR2	Return by an overseas company subject to branch registration of an alteration to constitutional documents	21 days
BR3	Return by an overseas company subject to branch registration, for alteration of constitutional documents	21 days
BR4	Return by an overseas company subject to branch registration of change of directors or secretary or of their particulars	21 days
BR5	Return by an overseas company subject to branch registration of change of address or other branch particulars	21 days
BR6	Return of change of person authorised to accept service or to represent the branch of an overseas company or of any change in their particulars	21 days
BR7	Return by an overseas company of the branch at which the constitutional documents of the company have been registered in substitution for a previous branch	21 days

Companies registered in Scotland

Form number	Description	Filing period
410	Particulars of a charge created by a company registered in Scotland	21 days
413	Particulars for registration of a charge to secure a series of debentures	21 days
413(a)	Particulars of an issue of debentures out of a series of secured debentures	21 days

416	Particulars of a charge subject to which property has been acquired by a company registered in Scotland	21 days
417	Register of charges, alterations to charges, memoranda of satisfaction and appointments and cessations of receivers	21 days
419(a)	Applications for registration of a memorandum of satisfaction in full or in part of a registered charge	–
419(b)	Application for registration of a memorandum of fact that part of the property charged (a) has been released from the charge or (b) no longer forms part of the company property	–
466	Particulars of an instrument of alteration to a floating charge created by a company registered in Scotland	21 days

Appendix 5

Schedule of recommended retention periods

Note: recommendations are based upon statutory requirements and principles of 'best' practice for commercial and damage limitation reasons.

Type of document	Statutory minimum retention period	Recommended period of retention
Incorporation documents		
Certificate of Incorporation and certificates on change of name	N/A	Permanently
Certificate to commence business (public company)	N/A	Permanently
Memorandum and Articles of Association (originals and updated copies)	Permanently	Permanently
Printed copy of resolutions submitted to Companies House	Permanently	Permanently
Statutory returns, records and registers		
Annual return (copy)	N/A	Permanently
Return of allotments (copy)	N/A	Permanently
Directors' service contracts	6 years after cessation	6 years after cessation
Register of directors and secretaries (original)	Permanently	Permanently
Register of directors' interests in shares and debentures	Permanently	Permanently
Register of interests in voting shares	Permanently	Permanently
Register of charges	Permanently	Permanently
Register of documents sealed (if applicable)	N/A	Permanently
Share registration documents		
Register of members	Permanently	Permanently
Register of debenture and loan stock holders	N/A	Permanently/ 7 years after redemption of stock

Letters and forms applying for shares, debentures, etc.	N/A	12 years from issue, with a permanent microfilmed record
Renounceable letters of allotment and acceptances	N/A	originals for 12 years from renunciation, with a permanent microfilmed record
Renounced share certificates	N/A	As above
Contracts for purchase of own shares by company	N/A	10 years from date of contract
Share and stock transfer forms and letters of request	N/A	12 years after date of transfer, with permanent microfilmed record
Requests for designating or redesignating accounts	N/A	12 years after request, with permanent microfilmed record
Cancelled share/stock certificate	N/A	1 year from date of cancellation
Stop notices and other court orders	N/A	Permanently
Letters of indemnity for lost certificates	N/A	Permanently
Powers of attorney	N/A	Permanently
Dividend and interest payment lists	N/A	Until audit of the dividend payment is complete
Paid dividend and interest warrants	N/A	6 years after date of payment
Unpaid dividend records	N/A	12 years after dividend declared

Dividend and interest mandate forms	N/A	3 years from when the instruction ceased to be valid
Notification of address change by member	N/A	2 years after notification
Trust deed securing issue of debentures or loan stock	N/A	Permanently

Accounting and tax records

Accounting records (as required by CA 1985 s 222)		
• public company	6 years	10 years
• limited company	3 years	10 years
Annual report and accounts (signed)	N/A	Permanently
Annual report and accounts (unsigned)	N/A	Permanently (keep sufficient copies to meet requests)
Interim report and accounts	N/A	Permanently (as above)
Budgets, forecasts and periodic internal financial reports	N/A	5 years
Taxation records and tax returns	Inspection possible up to 6 years after tax/accounting period	Permanently
VAT records and Customs & Excise returns	Inspection may be conducted up to 6 years after period	Permanently
Expense accounts	N/A	7 years

Bank records

Cheques, bills of exchange and other negotiable instruments	N/A	6 years
Paying-in counterfoils	N/A	6 years
Statements from and instructions to bank	N/A	6 years after ceasing to be effective

Charity donation documents

Deeds of Covenant	6 years after last payment	12 years after last payment

Documents supporting entries in accounts for donations	3 or 6 years	6 years
Contracts		
Contracts executed under seal	N/A	12 years after expiry
Contracts with customers, suppliers, agents or others	N/A	6 years after expiry or contract completion
Rental and hire purchase agreements	N/A	6 years after expiry
Licensing agreements	N/A	6 years after expiry
Trust deeds and rules (pension schemes)	N/A	Permanently
Employee records		
Job applications and interview records	N/A	Up to 1 year
Personnel records	N/A	7 years after employment ceases, with permanent microfilm record
Senior executive records	N/A	Permanently
Training records	N/A	6 years after employment ceases
Employment agreements	N/A	Permanently
Payroll and wage records (including details on overtime, bonuses and expenses)	6 years	12 years
Salary records	N/A	5 years
Time cards and piecework records	N/A	2 years
Details of benefits in kind	6 years	12 years
Income tax records (P45, P60, P58, P48, etc)	6 years	12 years
Annual return of taxable pay and tax paid	6 years	12 years
Labour agreements	N/A	10 years after ceasing to be effective
Works council minutes	N/A	Permanently
Employee records from closed units	Some 6 years	12 years

Health and safety

Record of consultations with safety representative and committees	N/A	Permanently
Health and safety policy documents (old and revised copies)	Implied permanently by Health & Safety at Work etc. Act 1974 s 2(3)	Permanently
Assessment of risks under health and safety regulations (including routine assessment, monitoring and maintenance records for aspects in workplace such as air quality, levels of pollution, noise level, use of hazardous substances, etc.)	Until revised (Management of Health & Safety at Work Regulations 1992, SI 1992/2051)	Permanently (old and current copies)
Accident report book and relevant records/ correspondence	3 years from date of entry (Health & Safety at Work etc Act 1974 s 7)	Permanently
Medical records (generally):	N/A	12 years
• Radiation accident assessment	50 years	Permanently
• Radiation dosage summary	2 years from end of calendar year	Permanently
• Under Control of Lead at Work Regulations 1998 (replaced 1980 regulations)	2 years from date of last entry to be effective	Permanently
• Under Control of Asbestos at Work Regulations 1987	40 years	Permanently
• Under Control of Substances Hazardous to Health Regulations 1994 ('COSHH' Regulations)	40 years	Permanently

Insurance

Public liability policies	N/A	Permanently
Product liability policies	N/A	Permanently
Employers' liability policies	40 years	Permanently
Sundry insurance policies and insurance schedules	N/A	Until claims under policy are barred or 3 years after policy lapses, whichever is longer

Group health policies	N/A	12 years after final cessation of benefit
Group personal accident policies	N/A	12 years after final cessation of benefit
Claims correspondence	N/A	3 years after settlement

Intellectual property records

Certificates of registration of trade/service marks (current and lapsed)	N/A	Permanently or 6 years after cessation of registration
Documents evidencing assignment of trade/ service marks	N/A	6 years after cessation of registration
Intellectual property agreements and licences	N/A	6 years after expiry
Material with copyright protection:		
• Literary, dramatic and musical works	N/A	Life plus 50 years
• Artistic works, recordings, films, photos and broadcasts	N/A	50 years

Pension scheme documents (unapproved schemes)

Trust deeds and scheme rules	N/A	Permanently
Trustees' minute books	N/A	Permanently
Record of pensioners	N/A	12 years after cessation of benefit
Money purchase details	N/A	6 years after transfer or value taken
Pension scheme investment policies	N/A	12 years after cessation of benefit payable

APPENDIX 5

***Pension scheme documents (Inland Revenue
approved and statutory pension schemes)***

Pension fund accounts and supporting documents	6 years from date accounts signed	Permanently
Actuarial valuation reports	6 years from date report signed	Permanently
Inland Revenue approvals	N/A	Permanently

Property documents

Title deeds for property	N/A	Permanently or until sold or transferred
Leases	N/A	12 years after lease and liabilities under the lease have terminated

Appendix 6

Permitted transactions involving loans

Exemption	Description	Private company	Relevant company
Group transactions	Loans, quasi-loans and provision of guarantees or security for loans between companies within a group	Permitted (CA 1985, s336)	Permitted (CA 1985, s333)
Directors' expenses	Provision of funds in advance to meet expenditure director has incurred or is about to incur in the normal conduct of duties	Permitted provided: • either members' prior approval is obtained in general meeting; • or there is a condition that, if approval is not given at or before the next general meeting, funding will be repaid or used to discharge liabilities on the company within six months of the meeting (CA 1985, s337)	Permitted, provided: • prior approval detailed in the previous column has been obtained • any money advanced does not exceed £20,000 (CA 1985, s337(3))
Transactions in 'normal' course of business	Loans, quasi-loans and provision of guarantees where such activities are within the normal course of the company's business	Permitted, provided the terms and the amount offered are not more favourable than what would be offered to a person of similar standing in the normal course of business (CA 1985, s338)	Permitted, provided: • requirements of the previous column are met • the amount concerned does not exceed £100,000 Note: where the company is a bank, there is no upper limit on the amount (CA 1985, s338(4))

	Loans to facilitate purchase of and fund improvements to director's main residence	Permitted, provided: • the aggregate amount of the loan does not exceed £100,000 • such loans are available to employees and the terms offered to directors are not more favourable (CA 1985, s338(6))	Permitted, provided requirements in previous column are met
Short-term quasi-loans	An arrangement where the company pays an amount for the director pending reimbursement, e.g. use of a company credit card where the director reimburses 'personal' expenditure	Permitted, provided: • the company is reimbursed within two months of expenditure being incurred • aggregate amount does not exceed £5,000 (CA 1985 s332)	Permitted, provided provisions in previous column are complied with
Small loans	Loan not exceeding £5,000 for any purpose	Permitted (CA 1985, s334)	Permitted
Minor and ordinary business transactions	Entering into a credit transaction or providing a guarantee for such a transaction where the goods or services are supplied to the director	Permitted, provided the aggregate amount does not exceed £10,000 Note: where the credit transaction is in the normal course of business and the terms and level of credit offered are not more favourable than would be offered to a person in the normal course of business, there is no upper limit	Permitted in accordance with previous column's provisions

Appendix 7

Inspection of service contracts

Requirements of CA 1985 s318

Each written contract of service and any variation to it must be available for inspection by any member free of charge.

Copies of the contracts must be kept at either the registered office, the principal place of business or at the same location as the register of members.

The Registrar must be notified of the location or any change in the location unless the contracts have at all times been kept at the registered office.

The directors must make sure that such documents are open to inspection by members of the company without charge (CA 1985 s318(7)).

Non-members may be charged a prescribed fee for inspecting these documents in line with the Companies (Inspection and Copying of Registers etc) Regulations 1991 (SI 1991/1998).

Additional Stock Exchange requirements

From the date of notice of the AGM, copies of service contracts must be available for inspection by members during normal business hours up to close of the meeting.

Copies must be available at the location of the AGM for at least 15 minutes prior to and during the meeting.

Notice convening the AGM must contain a note either that service contracts are available for inspection or that no such contracts exist.

A statement must be made in the directors' report to the annual report and accounts, either stating the unexpired term of service contracts of any directors proposed for re-election at the AGM, or that no such contracts exist.

Appendix 8

Resolution types and requirements for notice and approval

Type of resolution	Period of notice required	No of votes at meeting required to be case in favour	Decisions requiring the resolutions
Ordinary resolutions	Determined by the type of meeting	Simple majority of votes of members present	Routine business, where CA 1985 or Articles state that approval is required by 'members in general meeting', such as alterations to the share capital (CA 1985, s121), providing authority for directors to allot shares, payment of a final dividend or capitalisation of reserves.
			Certain ordinary resolutions such as alterations to the share capital and renewal of directors' authority to allot shares must be submitted to the Registrar of Companies within 15 days of being passed (CA 1985, s380).
Extra-ordinary resolutions	Determined by the type of meeting	75% of votes of members present	All resolutions proposed at class meetings, as required by the Articles, a variation of class rights (CA 1985, s125(2)), grant of authority to the liquidator in a voluntary winding-up to compromise claims (IA 1986, s165(2)) and for voluntary winding-up (IA 1986, s84(1)).
			Must state resolution as an 'extraordinary resolution' in notice of meeting.
			Must file a signed copy with Registrar of Companies within 15 days of being passed (CA 1985, s380(4)(b)).

| Special resolutions (s378(2)) | 21 clear days' notice | 75% of votes of members present | As required by the Act or Articles, which will state where a special resolution is required, such as to alter provisions in the Memorandum and Articles, change the company's name, re-register the company, waive members' pre-emption rights, make a reduction of capital, approve financial assistance for a private company to purchase its own shares or ratify an act of the directors. The notice must state resolution as a 'special resolution'. Must file a signed copy with Registrar of Companies within 15 days of being passed (CA 1985, s380(4)(a)). |
| Elective resolutions (s379A, see note (iii) below) | 21 clear days' notice | 100% of all members entitled to attend and vote at the meeting | Provide authority to directors to allot shares for an indefinite period, reduce the majority required for agreement to meetings being held on short notice and to dispense with requirements to:
• lay accounts before members at general meetings;
• hold AGMs;
• appoint auditors each year.
Must file a signed copy with Registrar of Companies within 15 days of being passed (CA 1985, s380(4)(bb), inserted by CA 1989 s 116(3)). |

Notes
(i) 'Members present' in this context means members present in person or by proxy who are entitled to vote at the meeting.
(ii) Agreement to short notice for consideration of the resolutions may be obtained in a similar way as that obtained for meetings being held at short notice.
(iii) Elective resolutions only apply to private limited companies and will automatically cease to have effect if the company is re-registered as a public company.

Appendix 9

Basic contents of the written statement of employment

1 Names of employer and employee.*
2 Date employment commenced (and the period of continuous employment).*
3 Remuneration and intervals at which it is paid.*
4 Hours of work.*
5 Holiday entitlement.*
6 Sickness entitlement.
7 Pension and pension schemes.
8 Entitlement to notice (this may be by reference to current legal entitlement or terms of a collective agreement).
9 Job title or a brief job description.*
10 Where employment is not permanent, the period for which it is expected to continue or, where it is for a fixed term, the date when employment is to end.
11 Place of work or, if the employee is required or allowed to work in more than one location, an indication of this and of the employer's address.*
12 The existence of any relevant collective agreements that directly affect the terms and conditions of the employee's employment and details of the persons who entered into such agreements.

Notes
- Employment particulars may be given in instalments, the last of which must be provided within two months of the start of the employment. The items identified with an * above must be given in the first instalment.
- Where the employee is normally employed in the UK but will be required to work abroad for the same employer for a period of more than one month, the statement must also include details of:
  - how long they will be working abroad;
  - currency in which they will be paid;
  - any additional pay or benefits;
  - terms on return to the UK.
- Where there are no particulars to be given for any of the items covered in the statement, this will have to be indicated.
- The statement must include a note about the employer's disciplinary and grievance procedures (except where fewer than 20 people are employed) and state whether a pensions 'contracting-out certificate' is in force for the employment in question.
- The statement may refer employees to other accessible documents, which the employee must consult for details of pension schemes, sickness entitlement, disciplinary rules and grievance procedures.

Appendix 10

Data protection principles

1 Personal data must be fairly and lawfully processed.
2 Personal data shall be obtained only for specified and limited purposes, and shall not be further processed in any manner incompatible with those purposes.
3 The amount of personal data held shall be adequate, relevant and not excessive in relation to the purposes for which it is held.
4 Personal data must be accurate.
5 Personal data shall not be kept longer than necessary.
6 Personal data shall be processed in accordance with individuals' rights.
7 Personal data shall be secured against unauthorised or unlawful processing, accidental loss, destruction or damage.
8 Personal data must not be transferred to a country outside the European Economic Area without adequate protection.

Appendix 11

Duties once placed in liquidation

Duties to the liquidator
Where winding up is imminent, directors must not:
- conceal any company property or debt;
- fraudulently remove company property;
- conceal, destroy, mutilate, falsify or alter company's books or papers;
- make false entries in books or papers relating the company's property or affairs;
- fraudulently part with, alter or omit information from documents relating to property or affairs;
- pawn, pledge or dispose of company property on credit.

Penalty imposed on directors
Fine, imprisonment or both (IA 1986 s206).

When a company is placed in liquidation, the directors must return to the liquidator all property, books, papers and other documents and items in their possession (IA 1986 s234).

Fine, which will increase over time (IA 1986 s235(5)).

When the winding-up order has been issued, directors must ensure that they do not:
- make a gift, transfer or create a charge on company property;
- conceal or remove property of the company.

Fine, imprisonment or both (IA 1986 s207).

During the winding-up the directors have a duty to:
- discover and disclose to the liquidator all the company's property, any disposals and the value received;
- deliver all property, books and papers in their custody to the liquidator;
- inform the liquidator of a false debt proved in winding up;
- produce all necessary books and papers affecting or relating to the company's property.

Fine, imprisonment or both (IA 1986 s208).

Directors must ensure that all books, papers and documents relating to the company's property or securities remain in their original form and are not destroyed, altered or tampered with in any way.

Falsifying books with intent to defraud or deceive creditors is an offence, resulting in a fine, imprisonment or both (IA 1986 s209).

Any statement of affairs given to the liquidator by the directors must contain all relevant information.

Fine, imprisonment or both (IA 1986 s210).

All representations made by directors to creditors for their agreement or consent to matters relating to winding up must be correct.

Fine, imprisonment or both (IA 1986 s211).

Appendix 12

Matters for determining unfitness of directors
(CDDA 1986, s9(1A))

Matters applicable in all cases

- Misfeasance or breach of any fiduciary or other duty
- Misapplication or retention of, or any conduct by the director giving rise to an obligation to account for, any money or other property of the company.
- Responsibility for the company entering into any transactions liable to be set aside under Part XVI of the Insolvency Act (provisions against debt avoidance).
- Responsibility for any failure by the company to comply with provisions of the Companies Act in relation to keeping and retaining accounting records and registers of directors, secretaries and shareholders, making annual returns and registering charges created by the company.

Matters applicable where the company has become insolvent

- Responsibility for the causes of the company's insolvency.
- Responsibility for the company entering into any transactions or giving any preference.
- Responsibility for any failure by the directors of the company to call a creditors' meeting in a creditors' voluntary winding up.
- Failure by the director to: comply with obligations imposed by or under provisions of the Insolvency Act in respect of statements of affairs where the company is in administration, receivership or is being voluntarily or compulsorily wound up; attend meetings of creditors; deliver company property or co-operate with the liquidator.

Sources of further information

AIM Rules for Companies
  Downloadable from www.londonstockexchange.com/aim
Company Law Handbook (16th edn), Keith Walmsley,
  www.butterworths.co.uk
Company Secretarial Procedures and Precedents, David Venus,
  www.butterworths.co.uk
The Model Code
  See Chapter 16 of the UKLA listing rules (see below)
Rights and Duties of Directors 6th edition, Martha Bruce, Tolley –
  www.butterworths.co.uk
UK Listing Authority's listing rules and guidance manual
  Available from the Financial Services Authority, 25 North Colonnade,
  London E14 5HS, 020 7676 3298, www.fsa.gov.uk

ICSA Publishing

- *Company Secretarial Practice*, Keith Walmsley
- *The ICSA Company Secretary's Handbook* (4th edn) Douglas Armour
- *The ICSA Company Secretary's Checklists* (4th edn) Douglas Armour
- *The ICSA Handbook of Good Boardroom Practice* Barbara Cooper
- *The ICSA Insolvency Guide* Patrick Hartigan
- *One Stop Meetings*
- *One Stop Insurance*
- *One Stop Company Secretary (3rd edition)*
- *One Stop Health and Safety*
- *One Stop Director*

Available from www.icsapublishing.co.uk

ICSA Best Practice Guides

- *The Appointment and Induction of Directors*
- *Duties of a Company Secretary*
- *Establishing a Whistleblowing Procedure*
- *A Guide to Best Practice for Annual General Meetings*

- *A Guide to the Statement of Compliance*
- *A Short Guide to Retention of Documents*

Published by ICSA, available from the Information Centre, ICSA, 16 Park Crescent, London W1B 1AH, 020 7580, informationcentre@icsa.co.uk

ICSA Guidance Notes

- *Audit Committee – Terms of Reference*
- *Directors and Officers Insurance*
- *Electronic Communications Update*
- *Matters Reserved for the Board*
- *Nomination Committee – Terms of Reference*
- *Polls – Chairman's Obligations*
- *Proxy Instructions – Abstentions*
- *Remuneration Committee – Terms of Reference*
- *Electronic Communications Order 2000: ICSA's Guide to Recommended Best Practice*

Downloadable from www.icsa.org.uk/news/guidance.php

Web resources

- **Association of British Insurers**
  www.abi.org.uk
- **The Department of Trade and Industry**
  www.dti.gov.uk
- **Financial Services Authority**
  www.fsa.gov.uk
- **The Institute of Chartered Secretaries and Administrators**
  www.icsa.org.uk
- **The Information Commissioner**
  www.dataprotection.gov.uk
- **The Institute of Directors**
  www.iod.co.uk
- **The London Stock Exchange**
  www.londonstockexchange.com
- **National Association of Pension Funds**
  www.napf.co.uk

- **The Registrar of Companies for England and Wales**
  www.companies-house.gov.uk
- **UK Listing Authority**
  www.fsa.gov.uk/ukla

Index

(References in bold refer to material in Appendix 1)